AN ELEMENTARY GRAMMAR OF THE KANNADA, OR CANARESE LANGUAGE

AN ELEMENTARY GRAMMAR OF THE KANNADA, OR CANARESE LANGUAGE;

IN WHICH

EVERY WORD USED IN THE EXAMPLES IS LITERALLY TRANSLATED

AND

THE PRONUNCIATION IS GIVEN IN ENGLISH CHARACTERS

BY

THOMAS HODSON,
WESLEYAN MISSIONARY

GYAN

Published by

Gyan Publishing House
5, Ansari Road
Daryaganj, New Delhi-110002
Phone: 011-47034999, 9811692060
E-mail: books@gyanbooks.com

Distribution Network
gyanbooks.com
India, USA, Canada, UK, Australia, France

ISBN : 978-81-212-4307-0 (PB)
First Published, 1859

2nd Impression 2020

Printed at: Gyan Press, Delhi.

An
Elementary Grammar
of the
Kannada, or Canarese Language
Author: Thomas Hodson

PREFACE.

The Tamil, the Telugu, and the Canarese, are the three principal languages of Southern India. The Canarese is spoken by several millions of Hindus who are living under the government of Englishmen.

To the Servants of the Government in the Civil, Judicial, and Educational departments, as well as to Missionaries, a knowledge of this language is absolutely necessary in order to a right discharge of their respective duties.

When the Author commenced the study of Canarese, he felt, as many others have done, the need of a short and plain introductory grammar. He therefore arranged, for his own use and improvement, the valuable but chaotic materials of McKerrell's grammar; and as he advanced in the language, he made various notes and additions. This manuscript, which was for years laid aside as useless, has now been carefully revised, and its contents are offered in their present form, as an elementary guide to those who wish to commence the study of this important language.

BANGALORE,
May 1*st* 1859.

CONTENTS.

SYNTAX.

APPENDIX.

THE ALPHABET.

1. In the modern Canarese alphabet, there are fourteen Vowels, thirty four Consonants, two letters which are either vowels or consonants, and one Compound letter.

2. Vowels.

Short ಅ *a*, ಇ *i*, ಉ *u*, ಋ *ṛi*, ಎ *e*, ಒ *o*.
Long ಆ *á*, ಈ *í*, ಊ *ú*, ೠ *ṛí*, ಏ *é*, ಓ *ó*.
Diphthongs ಐ *ai*, ಔ *ou*.

3. The following are either vowels or consonants: ಂ *m*, *n* or *ng*, according to position, and ಃ *aha*.

4. Consonants.

Twenty-five Classified *Consonants.*

	Unaspirated.	Aspirated.	Unaspirated.	Aspirated.	Nasal.
Guttural Class	ಕ *ka*	ಖ *kha*	ಗ *ga*	ಘ *gha*	ಙ *gna*
Palatal	ಚ *cha*	ಛ *chha*	ಜ *ja*	ಝ *jha*	ಞ *nya*
Cerebral	ಟ *ṭa*	ಠ *ṭha*	ಡ *ḍa*	ಢ *ḍha*	ಣ *ṇa*
Dental	ತ *ta*	ಥ *tha*	ದ *da*	ಧ *dha*	ನ *na*
Labial	ಪ *pa*	ಫ *pha*	ಬ *ba*	ಭ *bha*	ಮ *ma*

Nine unclassified *Consonants.*

ಯ *ya*, ರ *ra*, ಲ *la*, ವ *va*, ಶ *sha*, ಷ *ṣha*, ಸ *sa*, ಹ *ha*, ಳ *ḷa*.

The Compound Letter ಕ್ಷ *kṣha*, compounded of ಕ *ka*, and ಷ *ṣha*.

TABULAR VIEW OF THE ALPHABET.

5. Vowels.

Initial forms.	Medial and final forms.	Correspon-ding English Characters.	Power of the vowels.	Examples of Consonants and vowels united.
ಅ	–	*a*	*like a in about*	ಕ್ *and* ಅ *become* ಕ *ka*
ಆ	ಾ	*á*	— *a* „ *far*	ಕ — ಆ „ ಕಾ *ká*
ಇ	ಿ	*i*	— *i* „ *him*	ಗ — ಇ „ ಗಿ *gi*
ಈ	ೀ	*í*	— *ee* „ *deep*	ದ — ಈ „ ದೀ *dí*
ಉ	ು	*u*	— *oo* „ *wool*	ನ — ಉ „ ನು *nu*
ಊ	ೂ	*ú*	— *oo* „ *cool*	ಪ — ಊ „ ಪೂ *pú*
ಋ	ೃ	*ṛi*		ಬ — ಋ „ ಬೃ *bṛi*
ೠ	ೄ	*ṛí*		ಮ — ೠ „ ಮೄ *mṛí*
ಎ	ೆ	*e*	— *e* „ *met*	ಯ — ಎ „ ಯೆ *ye*
ಏ	ೇ	*é*	— *a* „ *mate*	ರ — ಏ „ ರೇ *ré*
ಐ	ೈ	*ai*	— *y* „ *my*	ಲ — ಐ „ ಲೈ *lei*
ಒ	ೊ	*o*	— *o* „ *not*	ಶ — ಒ „ ಶೊ *sho*
ಓ	ೋ	*ó*	— *o* „ *note*	ಸ — ಓ „ ಸೋ *só*
ಔ	ೌ	*ou*	— *ow* „ *owl*	ಹ — ಔ „ ಹೌ *hou*

6. Consonants.

Consonants with the inherent vowel ಅ *a*.	Corresponding English Characters.	Sound of the Consonants with the inherent vowel ಅ *a*.	Form and position when combined with other consonants.	EXAMPLES.	
ಕ	*ka*	like *ka* in *kalendar*	್ಕ	ಓಸ್ಕರ	*óskara.*
ಖ	*kha*	— * ,,	್ಖ	ಸ್ಖಲನ	*skhalana.*
ಗ	*ga*	— *ga* ,, *gander*	್ಗ	ಕಾಡ್ಗೋಣ	*káḍgóṇa.*
ಘ	*gha*	— * ,,	್ಘ	ಉದ್ಘಾಟ	*udgháṭa.*
ಙ	*gna*	— *gna* ,, *magnate*	್ಙ	ಶಾರ್ಙ್ಗ	*shárgna.*
ಚ	*cha*	— *cha* ,, *chapter*	್ಚ	ನಿಶ್ಚಯ	*nishchaya.*
ಛ	*chha*	— * ,,	್ಛ	ಇಚ್ಛೆ	*ichchhe.*
ಜ	*ja*	— *ja* ,, *jam*	್ಜ	ಕುಬ್ಜ	*kubja.*
ಝ	*jha*	— * ,,	್ಝ	ಜಝ್ಝಾರ	*jajhjhára.*
ಞ	*nya*	— *nya* ,, *banyan*	್ಞ	ಆಜ್ಞೆ	*ágnye.*
ಟ	*ṭa*	— *rta* ,, *martaban*	್ಟ	ಕಷ್ಟ	*kaṣhṭa.*
ಠ	*ṭha*	— * ,,	್ಠ	ಕೊಠ್ಠಡಿ	*koṭhṭhaḍi.*
ಡ	*ḍa*	— *rda* ,, *cardamom*	್ಡ	ಬಡ್ಡಿ	*baḍḍi.*
ಢ	*ḍha*	— * ,,	್ಢ	ಅಷಡ್ಢಾಳ	*aṣhaḍḍhála.*
ಣ	*ṇa*	— *rna* ,, *carnal*	್ಣ	ಪಟ್ಣ	*paṭṇa.*
ತ	*ta*	— *tha* ,, *thank*	್ತ	ಸಮಸ್ತ	*samasta.*
ಥ	*tha*	— * ,,	್ಥ	ಸ್ಥಳ	*sthaḷa*
ದ	*da*	— *tha* ,, *that*	್ದ	ತಾಳ್ದು	*táḷdu.*
ಧ	*dha*	— * ,,	್ಧ	ಆರಬ್ಧ	*árabdha.*
ನ	*na*	— *na* ,, *natural*	್ನ	ಪತ್ನಿ	*patni.*
ಪ	*pa*	— *pa* ,, *parrot*	್ಪ	ಅಣ್ಪು	*aṇpu.*
ಫ	*pha*	— * ,,	್ಫ	ಸ್ಫಟಿಕ	*sphaṭika.*
ಬ	*ba*	— *ba* ,, *barrow*	್ಬ	ಕಿಲ್ಬಿಷ	*kilbiṣha.*
ಭ	*bha*	— * ,,	್ಭ	ಅದ್ಭುತ	*adbhuta.*
ಮ	*ma*	— *ma* ,, *matter*	್ಮ	ಯುಗ್ಮ	*yugma.*
ಯ	*ya*	— *ya* ,, *yam*	್ಯ	ಹ್ಯಾಗೆ	*hyáge.*
ರ	*ra*	— *ra* ,, *ray*	್ರ	ಪ್ರಾಣ	*práṇa.*
ಲ	*la*	— *la* ,, *lack*	್ಲ	ಆಹ್ಲಾದ	*áhláda.*
ವ	*va*	— *va* ,, *van*	್ವ	ಬಿಲ್ವ	*bilva.*
ಶ	*sha*	— *sha* ,, *sham*	್ಶ	ಮತ್ಶಿರ	*matshira.*
ಷ	*ṣha*	— *rsha* , *marshal*	್ಷ	ವರ್ಷ	*varṣha.*
ಸ	*sa*	— *sa* ,, *sat*	್ಸ	ವತ್ಸ	*vatsa.*
ಹ	*ha*	— *ha* ,, *ham*	್ಹ	ಆಣ್ಹಿ	*áṇhi.*
ಳ	*ḷa*	— *rḷa* ,, *moorland*	್ಳ	ಕಟ್ಳೆ	*kaṭḷe.*
ಕ್ಷ	*kṣha*	— *kṣha* , *melksham*	್ಕ್ಷ	ತತ್ಕ್ಷಣ	*tatkṣhaṇa.*

* The preceding sound aspirated.

PRONUNCIATION.

7. 1st. Vowels.

The Vowels are pronounced according to the directions given in the preceding tabular view of the alphabet, except ಎ *e*, ಏ *é*, ಒ *o*, ಓ *ó*, which, when initial, are pronounced *ye*, *yé*, *wo*, *wó*; as, ಎಲ್ಲಾ *yellá*, ಏನು, *yénu*, ಒಂದು *wondu*, (Eng. one,) ಓಡು *wóḍu*. In ಋ *ṛi*, ೠ *ṛí*, the *i* and *í* have the short and long sound of the French *eu*.

8. 2nd. Consonants.

The following fourteen Consonants are pronounced like the English letters by which they are represented: ಕ *ka*, ಗ *ga*, ಚ *cha*, ಜ *ja*, ಪ *pa*, ಬ *ba*, ಮ *ma*, ಯ *ya*, ರ *ra*, ಲ *la*, ವ *wa or va*, ಶ *sha*, ಸ *sa*, ಹ *ha*.

9. The remaining Consonants do not correspond with the letters of the English alphabet. The following are Dental letters; they must be pronounced with the tip of the tongue between the front teeth: ತ *ta*, ಥ *tha*, ದ *da*, ಧ *dha*, ನ *na*.

If the learner be not careful in giving the Dental sound to the above five letters, his Canarese pronunciation will be like the English of a negro, who says, *dis*, *dat*, *dees*, and *dōze*, instead of *this*, *that*, *these* and *those*.

10. The following are Cerebral letters:—

ಟ *ṭa*, ಠ *ṭha*, ಡ *ḍa*, ಢ *ḍha*, ಣ *ṇa*, ಷ *ṣha*, ಳ *ḷa*.

There is a dot below the English representatives of these cerebral letters, to distinguish them from the dentals. They are pronounced with the tip of the tongue turned upwards, so as to touch the roof of the mouth, as far away from the front teeth as possible. This causes every letter of the cerebral class, especially when preceded by a long vowel, to commence with a slight sound of r. See the examples in the tabular view of the alphabet.

Unless the learner be careful to make a wide difference between the dental *t* and the cerebral *ṭ*, the dental *d* and the cerebral *ḍ*, &c. his pronunciation will be decidedly bad; he will often be unintelligible, and very frequently make the most ludicrous mistakes.

TABLE SHEWING THE ALPHABET WITH THE

ಅ *a*	ಆ *á*	ಇ *i*	ಈ *í*	ಉ *u*	ಊ *ú*	ಋ *ṛi*	ೠ *ṛí*
ಕ *ka*	ಕಾ *ká*	ಕಿ *ki*	ಕೀ *kí*	ಕು *ku*	ಕೂ *kú*	ಕೃ *kṛi*	ಕೄ *kṛí*
ಖ *kha*	ಖಾ *khá*	ಖಿ *khi*	ಖೀ *khí*	ಖು *khu*	ಖೂ *khú*	ಖೃ *khṛi*	ಖೄ *khṛí*
ಗ *ga*	ಗಾ *gá*	ಗಿ *gi*	ಗೀ *gí*	ಗು *gu*	ಗೂ *gú*	ಗೃ *gṛi*	ಗೄ *gṛí*
ಘ *gha*	ಘಾ *ghá*	ಘಿ *ghi*	ಘೀ *ghí*	ಘು *ghu*	ಘೂ *ghú*	ಘೃ *ghṛi*	ಘೄ *ghṛí*
ಙ *gna*	ಙಾ *gná*	ಙಿ *gni*	ಙೀ *gní*	ಙು *gnu*	ಙೂ *gnú*	ಙೃ *gnṛi*	ಙೄ *gnṛí*
ಚ *cha*	ಚಾ *chá*	ಚಿ *chi*	ಚೀ *chí*	ಚು *chu*	ಚೂ *chú*	ಚೃ *chṛi*	ಚೄ *chṛí*
ಛ *chha*	ಛಾ *chhá*	ಛಿ *chhi*	ಛೀ *chhí*	ಛು *chhu*	ಛೂ *chhú*	ಛೃ *chhṛi*	ಛೄ *chhṛí*
ಜ *ja*	ಜಾ *já*	ಜಿ *ji*	ಜೀ *jí*	ಜು *ju*	ಜೂ *jú*	ಜೃ *jṛi*	ಜೄ *jṛí*
ಝ *jha*	ಝಾ *jhá*	ಝಿ *jhi*	ಝೀ *jhí*	ಝು *jhu*	ಝೂ *jhú*	ಝೃ *jhṛi*	ಝೄ *jhṛí*
ಞ *nya*	ಞಾ *nyá*	ಞಿ *nyi*	ಞೀ *nyí*	ಞು *nyu*	ಞೂ *nyú*	ಞೃ *nyṛi*	ಞೄ *nyṛí*
ಟ *ṭa*	ಟಾ *ṭá*	ಟಿ *ṭi*	ಟೀ *ṭí*	ಟು *ṭu*	ಟೂ *ṭú*	ಟೃ *ṭṛi*	ಟೄ *ṭṛí*
ಠ *ṭha*	ಠಾ *ṭhá*	ಠಿ *ṭhi*	ಠೀ *ṭhí*	ಠು *ṭhu*	ಠೂ *ṭhú*	ಠೃ *ṭhṛi*	ಠೄ *ṭhṛí*
ಡ *ḍa*	ಡಾ *ḍá*	ಡಿ *ḍi*	ಡೀ *ḍí*	ಡು *ḍu*	ಡೂ *ḍú*	ಡೃ *ḍṛi*	ಡೄ *ḍṛí*
ಢ *ḍha*	ಢಾ *ḍhá*	ಢಿ *ḍhi*	ಢೀ *ḍhí*	ಢು *ḍhu*	ಢೂ *ḍhú*	ಢೃ *ḍhṛi*	ಢೄ *ḍhṛí*
ಣ *ṇa*	ಣಾ *ṇá*	ಣಿ *ṇi*	ಣೀ *ṇí*	ಣು *ṇu*	ಣೂ *ṇú*	ಣೃ *ṇṛi*	ಣೄ *ṇṛí*
ತ *ta*	ತಾ *tá*	ತಿ *ti*	ತೀ *tí*	ತು *tu*	ತೂ *tú*	ತೃ *tṛi*	ತೄ *tṛí*
ಥ *tha*	ಥಾ *thá*	ಥಿ *thi*	ಥೀ *thí*	ಥು *thu*	ಥೂ *thú*	ಥೃ *thṛi*	ಥೄ *thṛí*
ದ *da*	ದಾ *dá*	ದಿ *di*	ದೀ *dí*	ದು *du*	ದೂ *dú*	ದೃ *dṛi*	ದೄ *dṛí*
ಧ *dha*	ಧಾ *dhá*	ಧಿ *dhi*	ಧೀ *dhí*	ಧು *dhu*	ಧೂ *dhú*	ಧೃ *dhṛi*	ಧೄ *dhṛí*
ನ *na*	ನಾ *ná*	ನಿ *ni*	ನೀ *ní*	ನು *nu*	ನೂ *nú*	ನೃ *nṛi*	ನೄ *nṛí*
ಪ *pa*	ಪಾ *pá*	ಪಿ *pi*	ಪೀ *pí*	ಪು *pu*	ಪೂ *pú*	ಪೃ *pṛi*	ಪೄ *pṛí*
ಫ *pha*	ಫಾ *phá*	ಫಿ *phi*	ಫೀ *phí*	ಫು *phu*	ಫೂ *phú*	ಫೃ *phṛi*	ಫೄ *phṛí*
ಬ *ba*	ಬಾ *bá*	ಬಿ *bi*	ಬೀ *bí*	ಬು *bu*	ಬೂ *bú*	ಬೃ *bṛi*	ಬೄ *bṛí*
ಭ *bha*	ಭಾ *bhá*	ಭಿ *bhi*	ಭೀ *bhí*	ಭು *bhu*	ಭೂ *bhú*	ಭೃ *bhṛi*	ಭೄ *bhṛí*
ಮ *ma*	ಮಾ *má*	ಮಿ *mi*	ಮೀ *mí*	ಮು *mu*	ಮೂ *mú*	ಮೃ *mṛi*	ಮೄ *mṛí*
ಯ *ya*	ಯಾ *yá*	ಯಿ *yi*	ಯೀ *yí*	ಯು *yu*	ಯೂ *yú*	ಯೃ *yṛi*	ಯೄ *yṛí*
ರ *ra*	ರಾ *rá*	ರಿ *ri*	ರೀ *rí*	ರು *ru*	ರೂ *rú*	ರೃ *rṛi*	ರೄ *rṛí*
ಲ *la*	ಲಾ *lá*	ಲಿ *li*	ಲೀ *lí*	ಲು *lu*	ಲೂ *lú*	ಲೃ *lṛi*	ಲೄ *lṛí*
ವ *va*	ವಾ *vá*	ವಿ *vi*	ವೀ *ví*	ವು *vu*	ವೂ *vú*	ವೃ *vṛi*	ವೄ *vṛí*
ಶ *sha*	ಶಾ *shá*	ಶಿ *shi*	ಶೀ *shí*	ಶು *shu*	ಶೂ *shú*	ಶೃ *shṛi*	ಶೄ *shṛí*
ಷ *ṣha*	ಷಾ *ṣhá*	ಷಿ *ṣhi*	ಷೀ *ṣhí*	ಷು *ṣhu*	ಷೂ *ṣhú*	ಷೃ *ṣhṛi*	ಷೄ *ṣhṛí*
ಸ *sa*	ಸಾ *sá*	ಸಿ *si*	ಸೀ *sí*	ಸು *su*	ಸೂ *sú*	ಸೃ *sṛi*	ಸೄ *sṛí*
ಹ *ha*	ಹಾ *há*	ಹಿ *hi*	ಹೀ *hí*	ಹು *hu*	ಹೂ *hú*	ಹೃ *hṛi*	ಹೄ *hṛí*
ಳ *ḷa*	ಳಾ *ḷá*	ಳಿ *ḷi*	ಳೀ *ḷí*	ಳು *ḷu*	ಳೂ *ḷú*	ಳೃ *ḷṛi*	ಳೄ *ḷṛí*
ಕ್ಷ *kṣha*	ಕ್ಷಾ *kṣhá*	ಕ್ಷಿ *kṣhi*	ಕ್ಷೀ *kṣhí*	ಕ್ಷು *kṣhu*	ಕ್ಷೂ *kṣhú*	ಕ್ಷೃ *kṣhṛi*	ಕ್ಷೄ *kṣhṛí*

COMBINATIONS OF THE VOWELS AND CONSONANTS.

ಎ *e*	ಏ *é*	ಐ *ei*	ಒ *o*	ಓ *ó*	ಔ *ou*	ಂ *am*	ಃ *aha*	
ಕೆ *ke*	ಕೇ *ké*	ಕೈ *kei*	ಕೊ *ko*	ಕೋ *kó*	ಕೌ *kou*	ಕಂ *kam*	ಕಃ *kaha*	ಕ *k*
ಖೆ *khe*	ಖೇ *khé*	ಖೈ *khei*	ಖೊ *kho*	ಖೋ *khó*	ಖೌ *khou*	ಖಂ *kham*	ಖಃ *khaha*	ಖ *kh*
ಗೆ *ge*	ಗೇ *gé*	ಗೈ *gei*	ಗೊ *go*	ಗೋ *gó*	ಗೌ *gou*	ಗಂ *gam*	ಗಃ *gaha*	ಗ *g*
ಘೆ *ghe*	ಘೇ *ghé*	ಘೈ *ghei*	ಘೊ *gho*	ಘೋ *ghó*	ಘೌ *ghou*	ಘಂ *gham*	ಘಃ *ghaha*	ಘ *gh*
ಙೆ *gne*	ಙೇ *gné*	ಙೈ *gnei*	ಙೊ *gno*	ಙೋ *gnó*	ಙೌ *gnou*	ಙಂ *gnam*	ಙಃ *gnaha*	ಙ *gn*
ಚೆ *che*	ಚೇ *ché*	ಚೈ *chei*	ಚೊ *cho*	ಚೋ *chó*	ಚೌ *chou*	ಚಂ *cham*	ಚಃ *chaha*	ಚ *ch*
ಛೆ *chhe*	ಛೇ *chhé*	ಛೈ *chhei*	ಛೊ *chho*	ಛೋ *chhó*	ಛೌ *chhou*	ಛಂ *chham*	ಛಃ *chhaha*	ಛ *chh*
ಜೆ *je*	ಜೇ *jé*	ಜೈ *jei*	ಜೊ *jo*	ಜೋ *jó*	ಜೌ *jou*	ಜಂ *jam*	ಜಃ *jaha*	ಜ *j*
ಝೆ *jhe*	ಝೇ *jhé*	ಝೈ *jhei*	ಝೊ *jho*	ಝೋ *jhó*	ಝೌ *jhou*	ಝಂ *jham*	ಝಃ *jhaha*	ಝ *jh*
ಞೆ *nye*	ಞೇ *nyé*	ಞೈ *nyei*	ಞೊ *nyo*	ಞೋ *nyó*	ಞೌ *nyou*	ಞಂ *nyam*	ಞಃ *nyaha*	ಞ *ny*
ಟೆ *ṭe*	ಟೇ *ṭé*	ಟೈ *ṭei*	ಟೊ *ṭo*	ಟೋ *ṭó*	ಟೌ *ṭou*	ಟಂ *ṭam*	ಟಃ *ṭaha*	ಟ *ṭ*
ಠೆ *ṭhe*	ಠೇ *ṭhé*	ಠೈ *ṭhei*	ಠೊ *ṭho*	ಠೋ *ṭhó*	ಠೌ *ṭhou*	ಠಂ *ṭham*	ಠಃ *ṭhaha*	ಠ *ṭh*
ಡೆ *ḍe*	ಡೇ *ḍé*	ಡೈ *ḍei*	ಡೊ *ḍo*	ಡೋ *ḍó*	ಡೌ *ḍou*	ಡಂ *ḍam*	ಡಃ *ḍaha*	ಡ *ḍ*
ಢೆ *ḍhe*	ಢೇ *ḍhé*	ಢೈ *ḍhei*	ಢೊ *ḍho*	ಢೋ *ḍhó*	ಢೌ *ḍhou*	ಢಂ *ḍham*	ಢಃ *ḍhaha*	ಢ *ḍh*
ಣೆ *ṇe*	ಣೇ *ṇé*	ಣೈ *ṇei*	ಣೊ *ṇo*	ಣೋ *ṇó*	ಣೌ *ṇou*	ಣಂ *ṇam*	ಣಃ *ṇaha*	ಣ *ṇ*
ತೆ *te*	ತೇ *té*	ತೈ *tei*	ತೊ *to*	ತೋ *tó*	ತೌ *tou*	ತಂ *tam*	ತಃ *taha*	ತ *t*
ಥೆ *the*	ಥೇ *thé*	ಥೈ *thei*	ಥೊ *tho*	ಥೋ *thó*	ಥೌ *thou*	ಥಂ *tham*	ಥಃ *thaha*	ಥ *th*
ದೆ *de*	ದೇ *dé*	ದೈ *dei*	ದೊ *do*	ದೋ *dó*	ದೌ *dou*	ದಂ *dam*	ದಃ *daha*	ದ *d*
ಧೆ *dhe*	ಧೇ *dhé*	ಧೈ *dhei*	ಧೊ *dho*	ಧೋ *dhó*	ಧೌ *dhou*	ಧಂ *dham*	ಧಃ *dhaha*	ಧ *dh*
ನೆ *ne*	ನೇ *né*	ನೈ *nei*	ನೊ *no*	ನೋ *nó*	ನೌ *nou*	ನಂ *nam*	ನಃ *naha*	ನ *n*
ಪೆ *pe*	ಪೇ *pé*	ಪೈ *pei*	ಪೊ *po*	ಪೋ *pó*	ಪೌ *pou*	ಪಂ *pam*	ಪಃ *paha*	ಪ *p*
ಫೆ *phe*	ಫೇ *phé*	ಫೈ *phei*	ಫೊ *pho*	ಫೋ *phó*	ಫೌ *phou*	ಫಂ *pham*	ಫಃ *phaha*	ಫ *ph*
ಬೆ *be*	ಬೇ *bé*	ಬೈ *bei*	ಬೊ *bo*	ಬೋ *bó*	ಬೌ *bou*	ಬಂ *bam*	ಬಃ *baha*	ಬ *b*
ಭೆ *bhe*	ಭೇ *bhé*	ಭೈ *bhei*	ಭೊ *bho*	ಭೋ *bhó*	ಭೌ *bhou*	ಭಂ *bham*	ಭಃ *bhaha*	ಭ *bh*
ಮೆ *me*	ಮೇ *mé*	ಮೈ *mei*	ಮೊ *mo*	ಮೋ *mó*	ಮೌ *mou*	ಮಂ *mam*	ಮಃ *maha*	ಮ *m*
ಯೆ *ye*	ಯೇ *yé*	ಯೈ *yei*	ಯೊ *yo*	ಯೋ *yó*	ಯೌ *you*	ಯಂ *yam*	ಯಃ *yaha*	ಯ *y*
ರೆ *re*	ರೇ *ré*	ರೈ *rei*	ರೊ *ro*	ರೋ *ró*	ರೌ *rou*	ರಂ *ram*	ರಃ *raha*	ರ *r*
ಲೆ *le*	ಲೇ *lé*	ಲೈ *lei*	ಲೊ *lo*	ಲೋ *ló*	ಲೌ *lou*	ಲಂ *lam*	ಲಃ *laha*	ಲ *l*
ವೆ *ve*	ವೇ *vé*	ವೈ *vei*	ವೊ *vo*	ವೋ *vó*	ವೌ *vou*	ವಂ *vam*	ವಃ *vaha*	ವ *v*
ಶೆ *she*	ಶೇ *shé*	ಶೈ *shei*	ಶೊ *sho*	ಶೋ *shó*	ಶೌ *shou*	ಶಂ *sham*	ಶಃ *shaha*	ಶ *sh*
ಷೆ *ṣhe*	ಷೇ *ṣhé*	ಷೈ *ṣhei*	ಷೊ *ṣho*	ಷೋ *ṣhó*	ಷೌ *ṣhou*	ಷಂ *ṣham*	ಷಃ *ṣhaha*	ಷ *ṣh*
ಸೆ *se*	ಸೇ *sé*	ಸೈ *sei*	ಸೊ *so*	ಸೋ *só*	ಸೌ *sou*	ಸಂ *sam*	ಸಃ *saha*	ಸ *s*
ಹೆ *he*	ಹೇ *hé*	ಹೈ *hei*	ಹೊ *ho*	ಹೋ *hó*	ಹೌ *hou*	ಹಂ *ham*	ಹಃ *haha*	ಹ *h*
ಳೆ *ḷe*	ಳೇ *ḷé*	ಳೈ *ḷei*	ಳೊ *ḷo*	ಳೋ *ḷó*	ಳೌ *ḷou*	ಳಂ *ḷam*	ಳಃ *ḷaha*	ಳ *ḷ*
ಕ್ಷೆ *kṣhe*	ಕ್ಷೇ *kṣhé*	ಕ್ಷೈ *kṣhei*	ಕ್ಷೊ *kṣho*	ಕ್ಷೋ *kṣhó*	ಕ್ಷೌ *kṣhou*	ಕ್ಷಂ *kṣham*	ಕ್ಷಃ *kṣhaha*	ಕ್ಷ *kṣh*

SYLLABLES.

11. The short vowel ಅ *a* is inherent in the initial or complete form of every consonant; so that every letter is capable of being a complete syllable. Thus, ಅವನ *a-va-na,* of him; ಅವಳ *a-va-ḷa,* of her; ಅವರ *a-va-ra,* of them; ಅದರ *a-da-ra,* of it.

12. The inherent vowel may be cut off by placing the mark ್ on the upper part of the consonant; thus, ರ *ra* becomes ರ್ *r,* ವ *va* becomes ವ್ *v,* &c. The consonant so deprived, is called a half letter.

The inherent vowel is also cut off when its consonant is placed below the line, or under another consonant, in the formation of a syllable; thus, ಪ್ರ *pra,* ಗ್ಲ *gla,* ದ್ವ *dwa,* ಸ್ನ *sna,* &c.

13. When a syllable is formed of two or more consonants, and one vowel, the vowel is always joined to the first or uppermost consonant, but sounded after the last or lowest one; thus, ಕ್ಲಿ *kli,* ತ್ಯು *tyu,* ಸ್ತ್ರೀ *strí.*

14. The half letter ರ್ *r,* is pronounced before the letter or syllable which, in writing, precedes it; thus, ವರ್ಗ *warga,* ಕರ್ತನು *kartanu,* ಹೊರ್ತಾಗಿ *hortági.*

SANDHI, OR THE UNION OF WORDS.

This occasions the elision, insertion, and permutation of letters.

A VOWEL CUT OFF, OR A HALF LETTER INSERTED.

The following observations will save the learner some perplexity in the compounding of words, the declension of nouns, and the conjugation of verbs.

15. When a word ending in ಅ *a,* ಇ *i,* ಈ *í,* ಉ *u,* or ಎ *e,* is followed by an affix commencing with a vowel, euphony requires the following changes; viz.

16. First, The terminating ಅ *a,* is cut off. Thus ಕುರುಬ *kuruba,* and the plural affix ಅರು *aru,* become ಕುರುಬರು *kurubaru,* shepherds. See 1st Declension. ಮಾಡುತ್ತ *máḍutta* and ಏನೆ *éne,* become ಮಾಡುತ್ತೇನೆ *máḍutténe,* I do. See 1st Conjugation.

17. Second, The terminating ಅ *a* may be cut off, or ಯ್ *y* may be inserted. Thus, ಮಾಡುತ್ತ *máḍutta* and ಇದ್ದನು *iddanu,* become ಮಾಡುತ್ತಿದ್ದನು *máḍuttiddanu,* or ಮಾಡುತ್ತಾ ಯಿದ್ದನು *máḍuttá yiddanu,* he was doing. See 1st Conjugation.

18. Third, The terminating ಇ *i* may be cut off, or ಯ್ *y* may be inserted. Thus, ಮಾಡಿ *máḍi* and ಇದ್ಧಾನೆ *iddháne,* become ಮಾಡಿದ್ಧಾನೆ *máḍidháne,* or

ಮಾಡಿ ಯಿದ್ದಾನೆ *mádi yiddháne,* he has done. See 1st Conjugation. ಕುರಿ *kuri,* and the affix ಉ *u,* become ಕುರಿಯು *kuriyu,* &c. See 3rd Declension.

19. Fourth, The terminating ಈ *í* requires the insertion of ಯ *y* before a vowel. Thus, ಸ್ತ್ರೀ *strí,* and the termination ಇಂದ *inda,* become ಸ್ತ್ರೀಯಿಂದ *stríyinda,* by a woman. See 3rd Declension.

20. Fifth, The terminating ಉ *u* is cut off before many affixes in the conjugation of verbs. Thus, ಮಾಡು *mádu* and ಉತ್ತ *utta,* become ಮಾಡುತ್ತ *mádutta,* doing, (See 1st Conjugation.) ಕೂಸು *kúsu,* and the accusative termination ಅನ್ನು *annu,* become ಕೂಸನ್ನು *kúsannu,* a child. See 4th Declension.

Sometimes ವ *v* is inserted; as ಗುರು *guru* and the accusative termination ಅನ್ನು *annu,* become ಗುರುವನ್ನು *guruvannu,* a priest. See 1st example, 4th Declension.

21. Sixth, The terminating ಎ *e* generally requires the insertion of ಯ *y.* Thus, ಧೊರೆ *dhore* and ಇಂದ *inda,* become ಧೊರೆಯಿಂದ *dhoreyinda,* by a master. See 3rd Declension.

Consonants Changed.

22. When a word ending in any vowel is followed by a word or affix commencing with ಕ *ka,* or ತ *ta,* the ಕ *ka* often becomes ಗ *ga;* and the ತ *ta* becomes ದ *da.* Thus, ಮರ *mara* and ಕಾಲು *kálu,* become ಮರಗಾಲು *maragálu,* a wooden leg. ಹುಲಿ *huli* and ತೊಗಲು *togalu,* become ಹುಲಿದೊಗಲು *hulidogalu,* a tiger's skin.

23. When a relative participle ending in ದ *da,* is compounded with the pronoun ಅದು *adu,* it, the final ಅ *a* of the participle, and the initial ಅ *a* of the pronoun are both cut off, and the ದ doubled; thus, ಕೇಳಿದ *kéḷida* who or which heard, and ಅದು *adu,* it, become ಕೇಳಿದ್ದು *kéḷiddu,* that which (any one) heard. ಕೇಳದ *kéḷada,* who or which did not hear, and ಅದು *adu,* become ಕೇಳದ್ದು *kéḷaddu,* that which (any one) did not hear.

24. When the past relative participle is irregular, and ends in ಟ್ಟ *ṭṭa,* the final or inherent ಅ *a* is cut off, and the ದ *da* of the pronoun is doubled. Thus, ಪಟ್ಟ *paṭṭa,* who or which experienced, and ಅದು *adu,* become ಪಟ್ಟದ್ದು *paṭṭaddu,* that which (any one) experienced or suffered.

PARTS OF SPEECH.

25. There are eight Parts of Speech, viz. Noun, Adjective, Pronoun, Verb, Adverb, Postposition, Conjunction and Interjection.

NOUN.

26. There are, 1. Common nouns; as, ಹೂವು *húvu,* a flower. 2. Proper nouns; as, ತಿಮ್ಮ *Timma,* a man's name. 3. Verbal nouns; as, ಕೊಡೆಯು

ವದು *kuṇiyuwadu,* the act of dancing. 4. Derivative nouns: as, ಕುಂಬಾರ *kumbára,* a potter. 5. Compound nouns; as, ಮನೇ ಬಾಗಲು *mané-bágalu,* a house door. 6. Nouns of relationship; as, ಅಪ್ಪ *appa,* father.

27. VERBAL NOUNS are formed by adding to the roots of all verbs, ಉವದು *uvadu,* ವುದು *vudu,* or ಓಣ *óṇa;* thus from ಬರೆ *bare,* write, are formed ಬರೆಯುವದು *bareyuvadu,* ಬರೆವುದು *barevudu,* or ಬರೆಯೋಣ *bareyóṇa,* the act of writing.

28. Others are formed by adding ಇಕೆ *ike* to the root, with the changes required by *sandhi;* as, ಮಾಡು *máḍu,* to do, ಮಾಡುವಿಕೆ *máḍuvike* or ಮಾಡಿಕೆ *máḍike,* the act of doing. ಹಾಡು *háḍu,* to sing, ಹಾಡುವಿಕೆ *háḍuvike* or ಹಾಡಿಕೆ *háḍike,* the act of singing. ಬರು *baru,* to come, ಬರುವಿಕೆ *baruvike,* the act of coming. ಆಳು *áḷu,* to rule, ಆಳುವಿಕೆ *áḷuvike,* ಆಳಿಕೆ *áḷike,* or ಆಳ್ಕೆ *áḷke,* the act of ruling, dominion.

29. Some roots are used as verbal nouns without change, as, ಬದುಕು *baduku,* to live, the act of living, or livelihood.

30. DERIVATIVE NOUNS are formed by adding certain affixes to the crude form of nouns.

(1.) ಆರ *ára,* and ಕಾರ *kára* or ಗಾರ *gára,* denote the agent, doer or contant practice; as, ಕುಂಬ *kumba,* an earthen vessel, ಕುಂಬಾರ *kumbára,* a potter; ಮೋಸ *mósa,* deception, ಮೋಸಗಾರ *mósa-gára,* a deceiver; ತೋಟ *tóṭa,* a garden, ತೋಟಗಾರ *tóṭa-gára,* a gardener.

(2.) ವಂತ *wanta* denotes possession; as, ಬುದ್ಧಿ *buddhi,* wisdom, ಬುದ್ಧಿವಂತನು *buddhi-wantanu,* a wise man; ಧನ *dhana,* wealth, ಧನವಂತನು *dhana-wantanu,* a rich man.

(3.) ತನ *tana,* and ಇಕೆ *ike,* form neuter and abstract nouns; as, ಹುಚ್ಚು *huchchu,* foolish, ಹುಚ್ಚುತನ *huchchutana,* foolishness; ಹುಡುಗ *huḍuga,* a boy, ಹುಡುಗತನ *huḍugatana,* boyhood. ಬುದ್ಧಿವಂತ *buddhiwanta,* wise, ಬುದ್ಧಿವಂತಿಕೆ *buddhiwantike,* wisdom.

31. COMPOUND NOUNS may be formed by the union of two nouns; as, ಬೆಳ್ಳಿ ಹಣ *beḷḷi-haṇa,* a silver fanam, ಅಚ್ಚು ಕೊಟೆ a printing office.

Nouns are also formed from participles, by affixing the pronouns ಅವನು *avanu,* he, ಅವಳು *avaḷu,* she, ಅದು *adu,* it, ಅವರು *avaru,* they, (mas. and fem.) and ಅವುಗಳು *avugaḷu,* they (neut.), to the relative participles. Thus ಬರೆಯುವ *bareyuwa,* who or which writes, and ಅವನು *avanu,* he, form ಬರೆಯುವವನು *bareyuwavanu,* a writer; ಹಾಡುವ *háḍuwa,* who or which sings, and ಅವಳು *avaḷu,* she, ಹಾಡುವವಳು *háḍuwavaḷu,* a songstress. ಮಾಡುವ *máḍuwa,* who or which makes, and ಅವರು *avaru* they, ಮಾಡುವವರು *máḍuwavaru,* makers; ಮಾರುವ *máruwa,* which are sold, and ಅವುಗಳು *avugaḷu,* they, ಮಾರುವವುಗಳು *máruwavugaḷu,* the things which are sold. ಹೋದ *hóda,* who or which went, ಹೋದವನು *hódavanu,* he who went, ಹೋದವಳು *hódavaḷu,* she who went, &c.

32. LIST OF NOUNS OF RELATIONSHIP.

MASCULINE.	FEMININE.
ಮುತ್ತಪ್ಪ, ಮುತ್ತಾತ *mutt-appa, mut-táta*, great grandfather.	ಮುತ್ತಮ್ಮ, ಮುತ್ತಜ್ಜಿ *mutt-amma, mutt-ajji*, great grandmother.
ಹೆತ್ತಪ್ಪ, ತಾತ *hett-appa, táta*, grandfather.	ಹೆತ್ತಮ್ಮ, ಅಜ್ಜಿ *hett-amma, ajji*, grandmother.
ಅಪ್ಪ, ತಂದೆ *appa, tande*, father.	ಅಮ್ಮ, ತಾಯಿ *amma, táyi*, mother.
ದೊಡ್ಡಪ್ಪ *doḍḍ-appa*, father's elder brother; mother's elder sister's husband.	ದೊಡ್ಡಮ್ಮ *doḍḍ-amma*, mother's elder sister; father's elder brother's wife.
ಚಿಕ್ಕಪ್ಪ *chikk-appa*, father's younger brother; mother's younger sister's husband.	ಚಿಕ್ಕಮ್ಮ *chikk-amma*, mother's younger sister; father's younger brother's wife.
ಅಣ್ಣ *aṇṇa*, elder brother.	ಅಕ್ಕ *akka*, elder sister.
ತಮ್ಮ *tamma*, younger brother.	ತಂಗಿ *tangi*, younger sister.
ಮಾವ *máva*, father-in-law.	ಅತ್ತೆ *atte*, mother-in-law.
ಗಂಡ *gaṇḍa*, husband.	ಹೆಂಡತಿ *heṇḍati*, wife.
ಮಗ *maga*, son.	ಮಗಳು *magaḷu*, daughter.
ಅಳಿಯ *aḷiya*, son-in-law.	ಸೊಸೆ *sose*, daughter-in-law.
ಮೊಮ್ಮಗ *mom-maga*, grandson.	ಮೊಮ್ಮಗಳು *mom-magaḷu*, granddaughter.
ಮರಿಮಗ *mari-maga*, great grandson.	ಮರಿಮಗಳು *mari-magaḷu*, great granddaughter.
ಬೀಗ *bíga*, son's wife's father; daughter's husband's father.	ಬೀಗಿತಿ *bígiti*, son's wife's mother; daughter's husband's mother.
ಸೋದರಳಿಯ *sódar-aḷiya*, sister's son; wife's brother's son.	ಸೋದರಸೊಸೆ *sódara-sose*, a man's sister's daughter; a woman's brother's daughter.
ಷಡ್ಡಕ *ṣhaḍḍaka*, wife's sister's husband.	ನಾದಿನಿ *nádini*, a wife's or husband's sister.
ಭಾವ *bháva*, husband's elder brother; wife's brother; paternal aunt's son; maternal uncle's son.	ಸವತಿ *savati*, husband's other wife.
ಮೈದುನ *meiduna*, husband's younger brother; wife's elder brother; paternal aunt's son; maternal uncle's son.	ವಾರಗಿತ್ತಿ *wáragitti*, husband's brother's wife.
	ಅತ್ತಿಗೆ *attige*, husband's elder sister; wife's elder sister; paternal aunt's daughter; maternal uncle's daughter.
ಸೋದರಮಾವ *sódara-máva*, maternal uncle.	ಸೋದರತ್ತೆ *sódar-atte*, paternal aunt; maternal uncle's wife.

GENDER OF NOUNS.

33. Nouns are of three genders, Masculine, Feminine and Neuter.

34. Men and gods are masculine; women and goddesses feminine; animals and inanimate objects, neuter. The word ಗಂಡು *gaṇḍu,* male, is often prefixed to shew the male sex; as, ಗಂಡು ಕೂಸು *gaṇḍu kúsu,* a male infant; ಗಂಡು ಹುಲಿ *gaṇḍu huli,* a tiger; ಗಂಡಾಳು *gaṇḍáḷu,* a male servant or labourer.

35. The word ಹೆಣ್ಣು *heṇṇu,* female, is often prefixed to shew the female sex; as ಹೆಣ್ಣು ಕೂಸು *heṇṇu kúsu,* a female child; ಹೆಣ್ಣು ಹುಲಿ *heṇṇu huli,* a tigress; ಹೆಣ್ಣಾಳು *heṇṇáḷu,* a female servant or labourer.

36. The following are exceptions: ಕಳತ್ರ *kaḷatra,* and ದಾರ *dára,* wife; ಕೂಸು *kúsu,* ತೋಕ *tóka,* ಪಸುಳೆ *pasuḷe,* ಮಗು *magu,* ಮೊಗು *mogu,* and ಶಿಶು *shishu,* all signifying child; also ಜನ *jana,* a person or people, are neuter; as, ಕೂಸು ಹುಟ್ಟಿತು a child is born; ಜನ ಬಂತು the people have come.

37. The names of inanimate things personified, or regarded as divinities, are of the gender of those divinities; as, ಅನಿಲ *anila,* ವಾಯು *váyu,* wind, or the god of wind; ಗರುಡನು *garuḍanu,* the brahmany kite, a deity and the vehicle of Vishnu; ಶ್ರೀ wealth, or the goddess of wealth, &c, &c.

38. Masculine Derivative-nouns ending in ಅನು *anu,* become feminine by changing ಅನು *anu,* into ಇತಿ *iti,* as ಮೋಸಗಾರನು *mósagáranu,* a deceiver (mas.) ಮೋಸಗಾರಿತಿ *mósagáriti,* a deceiver (fem.)

39. The gender of the following nouns is denoted by different words.

ಗೂಳಿ *gúḷi,* a bull;	ಆಕಳು *ákaḷu,* a cow.
ಹೋರಿ *hóri,* a steer;	ಕಡಸು *kaḍasu,* a heifer.
ಕೋಣ *kóṇa,* a he-buffalo;	ಎಮ್ಮೆ *yemme,* a she-buffalo.
ಟಗರು *ṭagaru,* ಎಳಗ *yeḷaga,* a ram;	ಕುರಿ *kuri,* a sheep.
ಹುಂಜ *hunja,* a cock;	ಹೆಂಟೆ *heṇṭe,* a hen.
ಹೋತ *hóta,* a he-goat;	ಆಡು *áḍu,* a she-goat.

NUMBER OF NOUNS.

40. Nouns have two numbers, Singular and Plural.

41. The plural is formed by inserting ಅರ್ *ar,* ಗಳ್ *gaḷ,* or ಅರುಗಳ್ *arugaḷ,* between the crude noun and the affix for each case; so that the nominative plural may end in ಅರು *aru,* ಗಳು *gaḷu,* or ಅರುಗಳು *arugaḷu.*

42. Plural nouns of *relationship* terminate in ಅಂದಿರು *andiru,* or ಅಂದಿರುಗಳು *andirugaḷu*; as ಅಣ್ಣಂದಿರು *aṇṇandiru,* or ಅಣ್ಣಂದಿರುಗಳು *aṇṇandirugaḷu,*

elder brothers. ಮಗ *maga,* a son, is an exception; its plural is ಮಕ್ಕಳು *makkaḷu,* sons.

43. When the cardinal numbers are used in reference to persons, the word ಜನ *jana,* may be added to ಒಂದು *wondu,* one; and either ಜನ *jana,* or ಮಂದಿ *mandi,* to all the other numbers; thus, ಒಂದು ಜನ *wondu jana,* one person; ಎರಡು ಜನ *yeraḍu jana,* or ಎರಡು ಮಂದಿ *yeraḍu mandi,* two persons. For the ordinal and multiplicative numbers, See Appendix.

DECLENSION OF NOUNS.

44. There are four Declensions, which are distinguished from each other by the gender of the nouns and their terminations in the crude state.

45. Masculine nouns terminating in the crude state in ಅ *a,* are of the First Declension; Neuter nouns in ಅ *a,* are of the Second Declension. All nouns in ಇ *i,* ಈ *ī,* ಎ *e,* or ಐ *ei,* are of the Third Declension. All nouns in ಉ *u,* and all other terminations, are of the Fourth Declension.

CASES OF NOUNS. (147.)

46. Nouns have eight cases, which are formed by adding the following affixes to the *Crude State* of the noun.

The state of a noun without any affix is called its crude state. (148.)

The same affixes are added to pronouns. (70.)

Cases.	Affixes.	Signs.	
1. Nominative	ಉ *u,*	a	See 147.
2. Accusative	ಅ *a,* * / ಅನ್ನ *anna,* / ಅನ್ನು *annu,*	a	149, 150.
3. Instrumental	ಇಂದ *inda,*	by	151—155.
4. Dat. 1st Declension	ಇಗೆ or ಗೆ *ige,* or *ge*	to	156—170.
2nd. „	ಅಕ್ಕೆ *akke,*		
3rd. „	ಗೆ *ge,*		
4th. „	ಇಗೆ *ige,*		
(Dat. pl. all Declensions)	ಇಗೆ *ige,*		
5. Ablative	ದೆಸೆಯಿಂದ *deseyinda,*	from	171, 172.
6. Genitive	ಅ *a,*	of	173—193.
7. Locative	ಅಲ್ಲಿ *alli,*	in	194—197.
8. Vocative	ಏ *ē,* &c.	O!	198, 199.

* Instead of these accusative affixes, the final vowel of the crude noun is sometimes lengthened. See 150.

47. As the crude state of the Noun generally ends in a Vowel, and all affixes for the cases, except one form of the dative, begin with a vowel, it is necessary, in the declension of nouns, to insert certain letters between the noun and its affixes: these are made according to the Declension, Gender, Number, and Case of the noun. Thus,

ಅ *a*, becomes ಅನ್ *an*, before a vowel in the Sing. num. of the 1st. Decl.
ಅ *a*, becomes ಅವ್ *av*, and ಅದ್ *ad* do do 2nd.
ಉ *u*, may become ಇನ್ *in*, do do 4th.

The following table exhibits, at one view, all the letters and syllables which have to be inserted, both in the Singular and Plural numbers.

	SINGULAR.			PLURAL.	
	Nominative, Vocative, Accusative.	Dative.	Instrumental, Ablative, Genitive, Locative.	All cases. Masculine and Feminine.	Neuter.
1st Declension Masculine	ನ್ *n*,	ನ್ *n*, * or nothing	ನ್ *n*,	ಅರ್ *ar*, ಗಳ್ *gaḷ* or ಅರುಗಳ್ *arugaḷ*.	—
2nd Declension Neuter	ವ್ *v*,	—	ದ್ *d*,	—	ಗಳ್ *gaḷ*.
3rd Declension Any Gender	—	—	—	ಅರ್ *ar*, ಗಳ್ *gaḷ*, or ಅರುಗಳ್ *arugaḷ*,	ಗಳ್ *gaḷ*.
4th Declension Any Gender	—	—	ಇನ್ *in* †	—	ಗಳ್ *gaḷ*.

* The insertion in this case is optional. If inserted, the affix for the dative case must be ಇಗೆ *ige*; if omitted, the affix is ಗೆ *ge*.

† This syllable may be inserted or omitted at pleasure.

48. 1st DECLENSION, or Masculine Noun ending in ಅ *a*.

Crude noun, ಕುರುಬ *kuruba*, a shepherd.

	SINGULAR.	PLURAL.
No.	ಕುರುಬನು *kurubanu*, a shepherd.	ಕುರುಬರು * *kurubaru*, shepherds.
Ac.	ಕುರುಬನ *kurubana*, a, &c.	ಕುರುಬರ *kurubara*, ,,
	ಕುರುಬನನ್ನ *kurubananna*, ,,	ಕುರುಬರನ್ನ *kurubaranna*, ,,
	ಕುರುಬನನ್ನು *kurubanannu*, ,,	ಕುರುಬರನ್ನು *kurubarannu*, ,,
In.	ಕುರುಬನಿಂದ *kurubaninda*, by or from, &c.	ಕುರುಬರಿಂದ *kurubarinda*, by, from, &c.
Da.	ಕುರುಬನಿಗೆ *kurubanige*, to, &c.	ಕುರುಬರಿಗೆ *kurubarige*, to, &c.
	ಕುರುಬಗೆ *kurubage*, ,,	
Ab.+	ಕುರುಬನದೆಸೆಯಿಂದ *kurubana-deseyinda*, from, &c.	ಕುರುಬರದೆಸೆಯಿಂದ *kurubara-deseyinda*, from, &c.
Ge.	ಕುರುಬನ *kurubana*, of, &c.	ಕುರುಬರ *kurubara*, of, &c.
Lo.	ಕುರುಬನಲ್ಲಿ *kurubanalli*, in, &c.	ಕುರುಬರಲ್ಲಿ *kurubaralli*, in, &c.
Vo.	ಕುರುಬನೇ *kurubané*, O, &c.	ಕುರುಬರೇ *kurubaré*, O, &c.

49. 2nd DECLENSION, or Neuter Noun ending in ಅ *a*.

Crude noun, ಮರ *mara*, a tree.

	SINGULAR.	PLURAL.
No.	ಮರವು *maravu*, a tree.	ಮರಗಳು *maragaḷu*, trees.
Ac.	ಮರವ *marava*, a, &c.	ಮರಗಳ *maragaḷa*, ,,
	ಮರವನ್ನ *maravanna*, ,,	ಮರಗಳನ್ನ *maragaḷanna*, ,,
	ಮರವನ್ನು *maravannu*, ,,	ಮರಗಳನ್ನು *maragaḷannu*, ,,
In.	ಮರದಿಂದ *maradinda*, by or from, &c.	ಮರಗಳಿಂದ *maragaḷinda*, by or from, &c.
Da.	ಮರಕ್ಕೆ *marakke*, to, &c.	ಮರಗಳಿಗೆ, *maragaḷige*, to, &c.
Ab.	ಮರದದೆಸೆಯಿಂದ *marada-deseyinda*, from or by, &c.	ಮರಗಳದೆಸೆಯಿಂದ *maragaḷa-deseyinda*, from or by, &c.
Ge.	ಮರದ *marada*, of, &c.	ಮರಗಳ *maragaḷa*, of, &c.
Lo.	ಮರದಲ್ಲಿ *maradalli*, in, &c.	ಮರಗಳಲ್ಲಿ *maragaḷalli*, in, &c.
Vo.	ಮರವೇ *maravé*, O, &c.	ಮರಗಳೇ *maragaḷé*, O, &c.

---

* or Nom. ಕುರುಬರುಗಳು *kurubarugaḷu*,
Ac. ಕುರುಬರುಗಳನ್ನು *kurubarugaḷannu*, &c.

N. B. The names of animals, &c. terminating in the vowel ಅ *a*, are declined like ಮರ; except ಗರುಡ *garuḍa*, a kite; ಬಸವ *basava*, an ox; ಕೋಣ *kóṇa*, a he-buffalo; and ಕಮಠ *kamaṭha*, a tortoise; which are declined like nouns of the *first* declension.

50. 3rd DECLENSION.

1st Example. Masculine Noun ending in ಎ *e*.

Crude noun, ಧೊರೆ *dhore*, a master.

	Singular.	Plural.
No.	ಧೊರೆಯು *dhoreyu*, a master, &c.	ಧೊರೆಗಳು *dhoregaḷu*, masters.
Ac.	ಧೊರೆಯ *dhoreya*, a, &c.	ಧೊರೆಗಳ *dhoregaḷa*, „
	ಧೊರೆಯನ್ನ *dhoreyanna*, „	ಧೊರೆಗಳನ್ನ *dhoregaḷanna*, „
	ಧೊರೆಯನ್ನು *dhoreyannu*, „	ಧೊರೆಗಳನ್ನು *dhoregaḷannu*, „
In.	ಧೊರೆಯಿಂದ *dhoreyinda*, by or from, &c.	ಧೊರೆಗಳಿಂದ *dhoregaḷinda*, by or from, &c.
Da.	ಧೊರೆಗೆ *dhorege*, to, &c.	ಧೊರೆಗಳಿಗೆ *dhoregaḷige*, to, &c.
Ab.	ಧೊರೆಯದೆಸೆಯಿಂದ *dhoreya-deseyinda*, from or by, &c.	ಧೊರೆಗಳದೆಸೆಯಿಂದ *dhoregaḷa-deseyinda*, from or by, &c.
Ge.	ಧೊರೆಯ *dhoreya*, of, &c.	ಧೊರೆಗಳ *dhoregaḷa*, of, &c.
Lo.	ಧೊರೆಯಲ್ಲಿ *dhoreyalli*, in, &c.	ಧೊರೆಗಳಲ್ಲಿ *dhoregaḷalli*, in, &c.
Vo.	ಧೊರೆಯೇ *dhoreyé*, O, &c.	ಧೊರೆಗಳೇ *dhoregaḷé*, O, &c.

51. 3rd DECLENSION.

2nd Example. Feminine Noun ending in ಈ *í*.

Crude noun, ಸ್ತ್ರೀ *strí*, a woman.

	Singular.	Plural.
No.	ಸ್ತ್ರೀಯು *stríyu*, a woman.	ಸ್ತ್ರೀಯರು *stríyaru*, women.
Ac.	ಸ್ತ್ರೀಯ *stríya*, a, &c.	ಸ್ತ್ರೀಯರ *stríyara*, „
	ಸ್ತ್ರೀಯನ್ನ *stríyanna*, „	ಸ್ತ್ರೀಯರನ್ನ *stríyaranna*, „
	ಸ್ತ್ರೀಯನ್ನು *stríyannu*, „	ಸ್ತ್ರೀಯರನ್ನು *stríyarannu*, „
In.	ಸ್ತ್ರೀಯಿಂದ *stríyinda*, by or from, &c.	ಸ್ತ್ರೀಯರಿಂದ *stríyarinda*, by or from, &c.
Da.	ಸ್ತ್ರೀಗೆ *stríge*, to, &c.	ಸ್ತ್ರೀಯರಿಗೆ *stríyarige*, to, &c.
Ab.	ಸ್ತ್ರೀಯದೆಸೆಯಿಂದ *stríya-deseyinda*, from or by, &c.	ಸ್ತ್ರೀಯರದೆಸೆಯಿಂದ *stríyara-deseyinda*, from or by, &c.

	Singular.	Plural.
Ge.	ಸ್ತ್ರೀಯ *striya*, of, &c.	ಸ್ತ್ರೀಯರ *striyara*, of, &c.
Lo.	ಸ್ತ್ರೀಯಲ್ಲಿ *striyalli*, in, &c.	ಸ್ತ್ರೀಯರಲ್ಲಿ *striyaralli*, in, &c.
Vo.	ಸ್ತ್ರೀಯೇ *striyé*, O, &c.	ಸ್ತ್ರೀಯರೇ *striyaré*, O, &c.

52. 3rd DECLENSION.

3rd Example. Neuter Noun ending in ಇ *i*.

Crude noun, ಕುರಿ *kuri*, a sheep.

	Singular.	Plural.
No.	ಕುರಿಯು *kuriyu*, a sheep.	ಕುರಿಗಳು *kurigaḷu*, sheep.
Ac.	ಕುರಿಯ *kuriya*, a, &c.	ಕುರಿಗಳ *kurigaḷa*, ,,
	ಕುರಿಯನ್ನ *kuriyanna*, ,,	ಕುರಿಗಳನ್ನ, *kurigaḷanna*, ,,
	ಕುರಿಯನ್ನು *kuriyannu*, ,,	ಕುರಿಗಳನ್ನು *kurigaḷannu*, ,,
In.	ಕುರಿಯಿಂದ *kuriyinda*, by or from, &c.	ಕುರಿಗಳಿಂದ *kurigaḷinda*, by or from, &c.
Da.	ಕುರಿಗೆ *kurige*, to, &c.	ಕುರಿಗಳಿಗೆ *kurigaḷige*, to, &c.
Ab.	ಕುರಿಯದೆಸೆಯಿಂದ *kuriya-deseyinda*, from or by, &c.	ಕುರಿಗಳದೆಸೆಯಿಂದ *kurigaḷa-deseyinda*, by or from, &c.
Ge.	ಕುರಿಯ *kuriya*, of, &c.	ಕುರಿಗಳ *kurigaḷa*, of, &c.
Lo.	ಕುರಿಯಲ್ಲಿ *kuriyalli*, in, &c.	ಕುರಿಗಳಲ್ಲಿ *kurigaḷalli*, in, &c.
Vo.	ಕುರಿಯೇ *kuriyé*, O, &c.	ಕುರಿಗಳೇ *kurigaḷé*, O, &c.

53. 4th DECLENSION.

1st Example. Masculine Noun ending in ಉ *u*.

Crude noun, ಗುರು *guru*, a priest.

	Singular.	Plural.
No.	ಗುರುವು *guruvu*, a priest.	ಗುರುಗಳು *gurugaḷu*, priests.
Ac.	ಗುರುವ *guruva*, a, &c.	ಗುರುಗಳ *gurugaḷa*, ,,
	ಗುರುವನ್ನ *guruvanna*, ,,	ಗುರುಗಳನ್ನ *gurugaḷanna*, ,,
	ಗುರುವನ್ನು *guruvannu*, ,,	ಗುರುಗಳನ್ನು *gurugaḷannu*, ,,
In.	ಗುರುವಿಂದ *guruvinda*, by or from, &c.	ಗುರುಗಳಿಂದ *gurugaḷinda*, by or from, &c.
	ಗುರುವಿನಿಂದ *guruvininda*, ,,	

	Singular.	Plural.
Da.	ಗುರುವಿಗೆ *guruvige*, to, &c.	ಗುರುಗಳಿಗೆ *gurugaḷige*, to, &c.
Ab.	ಗುರುವದೆಸೆಯಿಂದ *guruva-deseyinda*, from or by, &c.	ಗುರುಗಳದೆಸೆಯಿಂದ *gurugaḷa-deseyinda*, from or by, &c.
	ಗುರುವಿನದೆಸೆಯಿಂದ *guruvina-deseyinda*, ,,	
Ge.	ಗುರುವ *guruva*, of, &c.	ಗುರುಗಳ *gurugaḷa*, of, &c.
	ಗುರುವಿನ *guruvina*, ,,	
Lo.	ಗುರುವಲ್ಲಿ *guruvalli*, in, &c.	ಗುರುಗಳಲ್ಲಿ *gurugaḷalli*, in, &c.
	ಗುರುವಿನಲ್ಲಿ *guruvinalli*, ,,	
Vo.	ಗುರುವೇ *guruvé*, O, &c.	ಗುರುಗಳೇ *gurugaḷé*, O, &c.

54. 4th DECLENSION.

2nd Example. Neuter Noun ending in ಉ *u*.

Crude Noun, ಕೂಸು *kúsu*, an infant.

	Singular.	Plural.
No.	ಕೂಸು *kúsu*, an infant.	ಕೂಸುಗಳು *kúsugaḷu*, infants.
Ac.	ಕೂಸ *kúsa*, an, &c.	ಕೂಸುಗಳ *kúsugaḷa*, ,,
	ಕೂಸನ್ನ *kúsanna*, ,,	ಕೂಸುಗಳನ್ನ *kúsugaḷanna*, ,,
	ಕೂಸನ್ನು *kúsannu*, ,,	ಕೂಸುಗಳನ್ನು *kúsugaḷannu*, ,,
In.	ಕೂಸಿಂದ *kúsinda*, by or from, &c.	ಕೂಸುಗಳಿಂದ *kúsugaḷinda*, by or from, &c.
	ಕೂಸಿನಿಂದ *kúsininda*, ,,	
Da.	ಕೂಸಿಗೆ *kúsige*, to, &c.	ಕೂಸುಗಳಿಗೆ *kúsugaḷige*, to, &c.
Ab.	ಕೂಸದೆಸೆಯಿಂದ *kúsa-deseyinda*, from or by, &c.	ಕೂಸುಗಳದೆಸೆಯಿಂದ *kúsugaḷa-deseyinda*, from or by, &c.
	ಕೂಸಿನದೆಸೆಯಿಂದ *kúsina-deseyinda*, ,,	
Ge.	ಕೂಸ *kúsa*, of, &c.	ಕೂಸುಗಳ *kúsugaḷa*, of, &c.
	ಕೂಸಿನ *kúsina*, ,,	
Lo.	ಕೂಸಲ್ಲಿ *kúsalli*, in, &c.	ಕೂಸುಗಳಲ್ಲಿ *kúsugaḷalli*, in, &c.
	ಕೂಸಿನಲ್ಲಿ *kúsinalli*, ,,	
Vo.	ಕೂಸೇ *kúsé*, O, &c.	ಕೂಸುಗಳೇ *kúsugaḷé*, O, &c.

NOUNS OF RELATIONSHIP.

55. Nouns of relationship require the insertion of ಅಂದಿರ್ *andir*, in the plural, between the crude noun and all other insertions and affixes. In other respects the nouns of relationship ending in ಅ *a*, are declined like nouns of the 1st declension, and those ending in ಇ *i*, or ಎ *e*, like nouns of the 3rd declension.

56. Crude noun, ಅಪ್ಪ *appa*, a father.

	SINGULAR.	PLURAL.
No.	ಅಪ್ಪನು *appanu*, a father.	ಅಪ್ಪಂದಿರು *appandiru*, fathers.
Ac.	ಅಪ್ಪನನ್ನು *appanannu*, ,,	ಅಪ್ಪಂದಿರನ್ನು *appandirannu*, ,,
	&c. &c.	&c. &c.

57. Crude noun, ಸೊಸೆ *sose*, a daughter-in-law.

No.	ಸೊಸೆಯು *soseyu*,	ಸೊಸೆಯಂದಿರು *soseyandiru*,
Ac.	ಸೊಸೆಯನ್ನು *soseyannu*,	ಸೊಸೆಯಂದಿರನ್ನು *soseyandirannu*,
	&c. &c.	&c. &c.

58. ಮಗ *maga*, a son, is an exception, and is declined as follows:—

No.	ಮಗನು *maganu*,	ಮಕ್ಕಳು *makkaḷu*,
Ac.	ಮಗನನ್ನು *maganannu*,	ಮಕ್ಕಳನ್ನು *makkaḷannu*,
	&c. &c.	&c. &c.

NOUNS OF QUALITY.

59. Nouns of quality of the *Neuter* Gender require the insertion of ಅರ್ *ar*, before the affixes for the Instrumental, Ablative, Genitive, and Locative cases. Thus,

ಕರಿದು *karidu*, a black thing.

	SINGULAR.	PLURAL.
No.	ಕರಿದು *karidu*,	ಕರಿಯವು *kariyavu*,
Ac.	ಕರಿದನ್ನು *karidannu*,	ಕರಿಯವನ್ನು *kariyavannu*,
In.	ಕರಿದರಿಂದ *karidarinda*,	ಕರಿಯವರಿಂದ *kariyavarinda*,
Da.	ಕರಿದಕ್ಕೆ *karidakke*,	ಕರಿಯವಕ್ಕೆ *kariyavakke*,
Ab.	ಕರಿದರದೆಸೆಯಿಂದ *karidara-deseyinda*,	ಕರಿಯವರದೆಸೆಯಿಂದ *kariyavara-deseyinda*,
Ge.	ಕರಿದರ *karidara*,	ಕರಿಯವರ *kariyavara*,
Lo.	ಕರಿದರಲ್ಲಿ *karidaralli*,	ಕರಿಯವರಲ್ಲಿ *kariyavaralli*,
Vo.	ಕರಿದೇ *karidé*.	ಕರಿಯವೇ *kariyavé*.

VERBAL NOUNS.

60. Verbal nouns ending in ಉವದು *uwadu,* require the insertion of ಅರ *ar,* before the affixes for the Instrumental, Ablative, Genitive and Locative cases in the Singular number. They have no plural.

61. ಮಾಡುವದು *máḍuwadu,* the act of doing.

No. ಮಾಡುವದು *máḍuwadu,*
Ac. ಮಾಡುವದನ್ನು *máḍuwadannu,*
In. ಮಾಡುವದರಿಂದ *máḍuwadarinda,*
Da. ಮಾಡುವದಕ್ಕೆ *máḍuwadakke,*
Ab. ಮಾಡುವದರದೆಸೆಯಿಂದ *máḍuwadara-deseyinda,*
Ge. ಮಾಡುವದರ *máḍuwadara,*
Lo. ಮಾಡುವದರಲ್ಲಿ *máḍuwadaralli.*

ADJECTIVES. (202.)

62. Adjectives precede the nouns to which they belong. Thus, ಹೊಸ ಬಟ್ಟೆ *hosa baṭṭe,* a new cloth; ಚಿಕ್ಕ ಗಿಡ *chikka giḍa,* a small shrub.

63. ಮರಿ *mari,* a young animal, is added to express the young of quadrupeds birds, fishes and insects; as, ಆನೇ ಮರಿ *áné mari,* a young elephant; ಕುದುರೇ ಮರಿ *kuduré mari,* a colt; ಕೋಳೀ ಮರಿ *kóḷí mari,* a chicken; ಇಲೀ ಮರಿ *ilí mari,* a young rat; ಮೀನು ಮರಿ *mínu mari,* a young fish; ಹಾವು ಮರಿ *hávu mari,* a young serpent.

64. ಕರು *karu,* a calf, is added to denote the young of cows and buffaloes only; as, ಆಕಳ ಕರು *ákaḷa karu,* a calf; ಎಮ್ಮೇ ಕರು *yemmé karu,* a young buffalo.

65. *Relative Participles* are used, before nouns, like adjectives, and in them the Relative Pronouns *who* and *which* are implied. Thus, ಹೋಗುವ ಮಾರ್ಗ *hóguwa márga,* the going road, the way in which he, &c. goes, or will go.

ಬಂದ ಮನುಷ್ಯನು *banda manuṣhyanu,* the arrived man, the man who has come.

ಮಾಡದ ಕೆಲಸ *máḍada kelasa,* the unperformed work, the work which he, &c. has not done, or will not do.

66. There are not many Adjectives in the Canarese language; the defect

is supplied by affixing to Nouns the irregular participles ಆದ *áda,* * and ಉಳ್ಳ *ulla.* ಅಂಥಾ *anthá,* such, is frequently added to these participles, as in the following examples:—ಬಲ *bala,* strength; ಬಲವಾದ *balawáda,* ಬಲವಾದಂಥ *balawádantha,* ಬಲವುಳ್ಳ *balawulla,* ಬಲವುಳ್ಳಂಥ *balawullantha,* strong, possessing strength. ಹಣ *haṇa,* money; ಹಣವುಳ್ಳ *haṇawulla,* ಹಣವುಳ್ಳಂಥ *haṇawullantha,* rich, possessing riches.

COMPARISON OF ADJECTIVES.

67. There is nothing in Canarese corresponding with the English *er* and *est, more* and *most,* by which adjectives can be compared. Comparisons are generally made by ಇಂತ *inta,* added to the dative case. The word ಇಂತ *inta,* signifies *than;* as ನನ್ನ ಕುದುರೆಗಿಂತ ನಿನ್ನ ಕುದುರೆ ದೊಡ್ಡದು *nanna kuduregínta ninna kudure doḍḍadu,* your horse is larger than mine.

ಎಲ್ಲಾ ಕುದುರೆಗಳಿಗಿಂತ ನಿನ್ನ ಕುದುರೆ ದೊಡ್ಡದು *yellá kuduregaligínta, ninna kudure doḍḍadu,* your horse is the largest of all. (161.)

68. Comparisons may be expressed by the dative and locative cases, without the addition of ಇಂತ *inta.* Thus, ನನ್ನ ಕುದುರೆಗೆ ನಿನ್ನ ಕುದುರೆ ದೊಡ್ಡದು *nanna kuduregé ninna kudure doḍḍadu,* to my horse, your horse (is) a large one; or, your horse is larger than mine.

ಎಲ್ಲಾ ಕುದುರೆಗಳಲ್ಲಿ ನಿನ್ನ ಕುದುರೆ ದೊಡ್ಡದು *yellá kuduregalalli ninna kudure doḍḍadu,* of, or among, all the horses, your horse (is) a large one; that is, your horse is the largest of all. (195, 196.)

PRONOUNS.

69. There are seven sorts of Pronouns, viz. 1. Personal. 2. Demonstrative. 3. Reciprocal. 4. Indeterminate. 5. Numeral. 6. Of quantity. 7. Interrogative.

N. B. There are no *Relative* pronouns in Canarese: they are implied in the relative participles. See paragraph 232. There are no Possessive

---

* ಆದ *áda,* who or which became, or has become, is the past relative of the verb ಆಗು *águ,* to be, become, &c. ಉಳ್ಳ *ulla,* who or which is, or possesses, is the relative participle of the defective verb ಉಂಟು *uṇṭu,* there is.

pronouns. Possession is expressed by the genitive case. (205.) Pronouns are declined like nouns.

I. PERSONAL PRONOUNS. (204—208.)

70. Crude state, ನಾ *ná*, I, (irregular.)

	SINGULAR.	PLURAL.
No.	ನಾನು *nánu*, I.	ನಾವು *návu*, we.
Ac.	ನನ್ನ *nanna*, me.	ನಮ್ಮ *namma*, us.
	ನನ್ನನ್ನ *nannanna*, „	ನಮ್ಮನ್ನ *nammanna*, „
	ನನ್ನನ್ನು *nannannu*, „	ನಮ್ಮನ್ನು *nammannu*, „
In.	ನನ್ನಿಂದ *nanninda*, by or from me.	ನಮ್ಮಿಂದ *namminda*, by or from us.
Da.	ನನಗೆ *nanage*, to me.	ನಮಗೆ *namage*, to us.
Ab.	ನನ್ನದೆಸೆಯಿಂದ *nanna-deseyinda*, from or by me.	ನಮ್ಮದೆಸೆಯಿಂದ *namma-deseyinda*, from or by us.
Ge.	ನನ್ನ *nanna*, of me, my.	ನಮ್ಮ *namma*, of us, our.
Lo.	ನನ್ನಲ್ಲಿ *nannalli*, in me.	ನಮ್ಮಲ್ಲಿ *nammalli*, in us.

71. Crude state, ನೀ *ní*, thou, (irregular.)

	SINGULAR.	PLURAL.
No.	ನೀನು *nínu*, thou.	ನೀವು *nívu*, ye or you.
Ac.	ನಿನ್ನ *ninna*, thee.	ನಿಮ್ಮ *nimma*, „
	ನಿನ್ನನ್ನ *ninnanna*, „	ನಿಮ್ಮನ್ನ *nimmanna*, „
	ನಿನ್ನನ್ನು *ninnannu*, „	ನಿಮ್ಮನ್ನು *nimmannu*, „
In.	ನಿನ್ನಿಂದ *ninninda*, by or from thee.	ನಿಮ್ಮಿಂದ *nimminda*, by or from you.
Da.	ನಿನಗೆ *ninage*, to thee.	ನಿಮಗೆ *nimage*, to you.
Ab.	ನಿನ್ನದೆಸೆಯಿಂದ *ninna-deseyinda*, from or by thee.	ನಿಮ್ಮದೆಸೆಯಿಂದ *nimma-deseyinda*, by or from you.
Ge.	ನಿನ್ನ *ninna*, of thee, thy.	ನಿಮ್ಮ *nimma*, of you, your.
Lo.	ನಿನ್ನಲ್ಲಿ *ninnalli*, in thee.	ನಿಮ್ಮಲ್ಲಿ *nimmalli*, in you.

II. DEMONSTRATIVE PRONOUNS. (Remote.)

72. Crude state, ಅವ *ava*, He, that man. (209.)
(used when speaking of an equal, or inferior.)

	Singular.	Plural.
No.	ಅವನು *avanu*, he.	ಅವರು *avaru*, they.
Ac.	ಅವನನ್ನು *avanannu*, him.	ಅವರನ್ನು *avarannu*, them.

&c. &c. like nouns of the 1st declension.

73. ಅವಳು *avaḷu*, (feminine of ಅವನು) She, that woman. (209.)
(used when speaking of an equal, or inferior.)

No.	ಅವಳು *avaḷu*, she.	ಅವರು *avaru*, they.
Ac.	ಅವಳನ್ನು *avaḷannu*, her.	ಅವರನ್ನು *avarannu*, them.

&c. &c. like the preceding example.

74. Crude state ಆತ *áta*, He, that man. (210.)
(used when speaking of a superior.)

No.	ಆತನು *átanu*, he.	ಆತಗಳು *átagaḷu*, they.
Ac.	ಆತನನ್ನು *átanannu*, him.	ಆತಗಳನ್ನು *átagaḷannu*, them.

&c. &c. like nouns of the 1st declension.

75. ಆಕೆ, *áke*, (feminine of ಆತನು) She, that woman. (210.)
(used when speaking of a superior.)

No.	ಆಕೆಯು *ákeyu*, she.	ಆಕೆಯರು *ákeyaru*, they.
Ac.	ಆಕೆಯನ್ನು *ákeyannu*, her.	ಆಕೆಯರನ್ನು *ákeyarannu*, them.

&c. &c. like nouns of the 3rd declension.

76. ಅದು *adu*, It, that thing. The syllable ಅ *ar*, must be inserted in the Instrumental, Ablative, Genitive and Locative cases *singular*.

No.	ಅದು *adu*, it.	ಅವು, ಅವುಗಳು *avu, avugaḷu*, they.
Ac.	ಅದನ್ನು *adannu*, ,,	(ಅವನ್ನು,) ಅವುಗಳನ್ನು *avannu, avugaḷannu*, them.
In.	ಅದರಿಂದ *adarinda*, by it.	ಅವುಗಳಿಂದ *avugaḷinda*, by them.
Da.	ಅದಕ್ಕೆ *adukke*, to it.	(ಅವಕ್ಕೆ,) ಅವುಗಳಿಗೆ *avakke, avugaḷige*, to them.
Ab.	ಅದರದೆಸೆಯಿಂದ *adara-deseyinda*, from it.	ಅವುಗಳದೆಸೆಯಿಂದ *avugaḷa-deseyinda*, from them.

Ge. ಅದರ *adara,* of it, its. ಅವುಗಳ *avugaḷa,* of them, their.

Lo. ಅದರಲ್ಲಿ *adaralli,* in it. ಅವಲ್ಲಿ, ಅವುಗಳಲ್ಲಿ *avalli, avugaḷalli,* in them.

DEMONSTRATIVE PRONOUNS. (PROXIMATE.)

SINGULAR.	PLURAL.
77. ಇವನು *ivanu,* he, this man.	ಇವರು *ivaru,* these men.
78. ಇವಳು *ivaḷu,* she, this woman.	ಇವರು *ivaru,* these women.

(used when speaking of equals or inferiors.)

79. ಈತನು *ítanu,* he, this man.	ಈತಗಳು *ítagaḷu,* these men.
80. ಈಕೆಯು *íkeyu,* she, this woman.	ಈಕೆಯರು *íkeyaru,* these women.

(used when speaking of superiors.)

81. ಇದು *idu,* it, this thing.	ಇವು, ಇವುಗಳು *ivu, ivugaḷu,* these things.

82. The above five pronouns are declined exactly like the five proceding ones. The Demonstrative *proximate* commence with ಇ *i,* and ಈ *í*; and the *remote* with ಅ *a,* and ಆ *á.* This is the only difference between them.

III. RECIPROCAL PRONOUN.

83. ತಾನು *tánu,* himself, herself, itself, is declined like ನಾನು *nánu,* I.

SINGULAR.	PLURAL.
No. ತಾನು *tánu,*	ತಾವು *távu,*
Ac. ತನ್ನನ್ನು *tannannu,* &c. &c.	ತಮ್ಮನ್ನು *tammannu,* &c. &c.

84. This pronoun is used with reference to some other noun or pronoun of the 3rd person preceding it. (211.)

The plural is used honorifically in the second person singular, in the sense of "your honor," "your Lordship," &c. when speaking to a person of rank. (212.)

IV. INDETERMINATE PRONOUNS.

SINGULAR.	PLURAL.
85. ಹೆರನು *heranu,* another man.	ಹೆರರು *heraru,* other men.

(declined like ಅವನು *avanu,* he.)

86. ಹೆರಳು *heraḷu,* another woman.	ಹೆರರು *heraru,* other women.

(declined like ಅವಳು *avaḷu,* she.)

87. ಹೆರತು *heratu,* another thing. ಹೆರವು *heravu,* other things.
(declined like ಅದು *adu,* it.)

88. The following have no Singular; they are declined like ಅವರು *avaru,* they.

ಕೆಲವರು *kelavaru,* some persons.
ಹಲವರು *halavaru,* several persons.
ಎಲ್ಲರು *yellaru,* all persons.

89. Their neuters are declined like ಅವು *avu,* or ಅವುಗಳು *avugaḷu,* those things.

ಕೆಲವು *kelavu,* some things.
ಹಲವು *halavu,* several things.
ಎಲ್ಲವು *yellavu,* all things.

V. NUMERAL PRONOUNS.

	SINGULAR.	PLURAL.
90.	ಒಬ್ಬನು *wobbanu,* one man.	ಇಬ್ಬರು *ibbaru,* two men.
	(declined like ಅವನು *avanu,* he.)	
91.	ಒಬ್ಬಳು *wobbaḷu,* one woman.	ಇಬ್ಬರು *ibbaru,* two women.
	(declined like ಅವಳು *avaḷu,* she.)	
92.	ಒಂದು *wondu,* one thing.	ಎರಡು *yeraḍu,* two things.
	(declined like ಅದು *adu,* it.)	

93. Other Numerals are declined in the same manner, viz. the Masculine and Feminine like ಅವರು *avaru,* they; and the Neuters like ಅದು *adu,* it.

VI. PRONOUNS OF QUANTITY.

94. Remote; ಅಷ್ಟರು *aṣhṭaru,* so many persons as *those,* } declined like
95. Proximate; ಇಷ್ಟರು *iṣhṭaru,* so many persons as *these.* } ಅವರು *avaru.*

96. Remote; ಅಷ್ಟು *aṣhṭu,* so much, or so many things as *those,* } declined like
97. Proximate; ಇಷ್ಟು *iṣhṭu,* so much, or so many things as *these.* } ಅದು *adu.*

VII. INTERROGATIVE PRONOUNS. (213.)

98. ಯಾವನು *yávanu,* who, what man?
ಯಾವಳು *yávaḷu,* who, which woman?
ಯಾವದು *yávadu,* which thing? with their plurals, are declined like ಅವನು *avanu,* ಅವಳು *avaḷu,* and ಅದು *adu.*

99. ಏನು *yénu*, what?

No. ಏನು *yénu*.

Ac. ಏನನ್ನು *yénannu*.

In. ಏತರಿಂದ *yétarinda*.

Da. ಏತಕ್ಕೆ or ಏಕೆ *yétakke* or *yéke*.

Ab. ಏತರದೆಸೆಯಿಂದ *yétara-deseyinda*.

Ge. ಏತರ *yétara*.

Lo. ಏತರಲ್ಲಿ *yétaralli*.

100. Some of the Demonstrative, Numeral, Local and other pronouns are abbreviated, or changed, when they form the first member of a Compound word.

101. The abbreviated forms of *one*, *two* and *three*, double the Consonant which follows them.

ಅದು *adu*, that, becomes		ಆ *á*.
ಇದು *idu*, this,	,,	ಈ *í*.
ಯಾವದು *yávadu*, which,	,,	ಯಾವ *yáva*.
ಒಂದು *wondu*, one,	,,	ಒ *o*.
ಎರಡು *yeraḍu*, two,	,,	ಇ *i*.
ಮೂರು *múru*, three,	,,	ಮೂ or ಮು *mú* or *mu*,
ನಾಲ್ಕು *nálku*, four,	,,	ನಾಲ್ *nál*.
ಐದು *eidu*, five,	,,	ಐ *ei*.
ಆರು *áru*, six,	,,	ಆರ್ *ár*.
ಏಳು *yéḷu*, seven,	,,	ಏಳ್ *yéḷ*.
ಎಂಟು *yeṇṭu*, eight,	,,	ಎಣ್ *yeṇ*.
ಒಂಭತ್ತು *wombhattu*, nine,	,,	ಒಂ *wom*.
ಹತ್ತು *hattu*, ten,	,,	ಹನ್ *han*, or ಹದಿ *hadi*.
ನಡುವು *naḍuvu*, middle,	,,	ನಟ್ *naṭ*.
ಮೇಗು *mégu*, upper,	,,	ಮೇ *mé*.
ಕೆಳಗು *keḷagu*, under,	,,	ಕೀಳ್ *kíḷ*.
ಹೊರಗು *horagu*, outside,	,,	ಹೊರ *hora*.
ಮುಂದು *mundu*, front,	,,	ಮುಂ *mun* or *mum*.
ಒಳಗು *woḷagu*, inside,	,,	ಒಳ *woḷa*.
ಹಿಂದು *hindu*, hinder,	,,	ಹಿಂ *hin* or *him*.

Examples.

ಅದು *adu*, and ಮನೆ *mane*, become		ಆ ಮನೆ *á mane*, that house.
ಒಂದು *wondu*, and ಕಣ್ಣು *kaṇṇu*,	,,	ಒಕ್ಕಣ್ಣು *wokkaṇṇu*, one eye.
ಹತ್ತು *hattu*, and ಒಂದು *wondu*,	,,	ಹನ್ನೊಂದು *hannondu*, eleven.
ಹತ್ತು *hattu*, and ಮೂರು *múru*,	,,	ಹದಿಮೂರು *hadimúru*, thirteen.

VERBS.

101. Verbs are divided into Active, Passive, Neuter, and Causal.

102. The root of the verb is generally the same as the 2nd per. sing. Imperative.

103. The roots of verbs generally terminate in ಉ *u*, ಇ *i*, ಎ *e*, or ಏ *é*.

104. There are two Conjugations, distinguished by the ending of the root of the verb. The 1st conjugation ends in ಉ *u*, and the 2nd in ಇ *i*, ಎ *e*, and other vowels.

105. There are four Simple Moods; viz. the Infinitive, the Imperative, the Negative, and the Affirmative. The Potential and the Subjunctive are compounds.

106. In the Affirmative mood there are four simple, and six compound Tenses.

107. The Infinitive mood is impersonal. The other simple moods and tenses are formed by adding certain personal affixes to the Root, to Gerunds, or to participles.

108. Two moods are formed by adding personal affixes to the root; two tenses by adding similar affixes to the present and past gerunds; and two other tenses by adding them to the past and future participles.

109. *The following are the personal affixes used in the Conjugation of Verbs.*

	IMPERATIVE.	NEGATIVE.	AFFIRMATIVE MOOD. Present Tense.	Past Tense.	1st Future Tense.	2nd Future Tense.
SINGULAR.						
1st Per.	ಅಲಿ *ali.*	ಎನು * *enu.*	ಏನೆ *éne.*	ಎನು * *enu.*	ಎನು * *enu.*	ಏನು *énu.*
2nd.		ಎ *e.*	ಈ *í,* or ಈಯೆ *íye.*	ಇ *i,* or ಎ *e.*	ಇ *i,* or ಎ *e.*	ಈ *í,* or ಈಯೆ *íye.*
3rd mas.	ಅಲಿ *ali.*	ಅನು * *anu.*	ಆನೆ *áne.*	ಅನು * *anu.*	ಅನು * *anu.*	ಆನು *ánu.*
3rd fem.	ಅಲಿ *ali.*	ಅಳು *aḷu.*	ಆಳೆ *áḷe.*	ಅಳು *aḷu.*	ಅಳು *aḷu.*	ಆಳು *áḷu.*
3rd neut.	ಅಲಿ *ali.*	ಅದು *adu.*	ಅದೆ *ade.*	ಇತು *itu.*	ಅದು *adu.*	ಈತು *ítu.*
PLURAL.						
1st.	ಅಲಿ *ali.*	ಎವು *evu.*	ಏವೆ *éve.*	ಎವು *evu.*	ಎವು *evu.*	ಏವು *évu.*
2nd.	ಇರಿ *iri.*	ಅರಿ *ari.*	ಈರಿ *íri.*	ಇರಿ *iri.*	ಇರಿ *iri.*	ಈರಿ *íri.*
3rd m. & f.	ಅಲಿ *ali,*	ಅರು *aru.*	ಆರೆ *áre.*	ಅರು *aru.*	ಅರು *aru.*	ಆರು *áru.*
3rd neu.	ಅಲಿ *ali.*	ಅವು *avu.*	ಅವೆ *ave.*	ಅವು *avu.*	ಅವು *avu.*	ಆವು *ávu.*

* ನು *nu,* may be omitted, except in the 2nd future tense. (222).

110. 1st CONJUGATION, or a Verb ending in ಉ *u*.

Root ಮಾಡು *máḍu*, Do. (102.)

Gerunds, or verbal participles. (223—231.)

		Compounded of the root and
Present.	ಮಾಡುತ್ತ *máḍutta*,	ಉತ್ತ *utta*.
	or ಮಾಡುತ್ತಾ *máḍuttá*, doing.	ಉತ್ತಾ *uttá*.
Past.	ಮಾಡಿ *máḍi*, having done.	ಇ *i*, *
Negative.	ಮಾಡದೆ *máḍade*, not having done.	ಅದೆ *ade*.

Relative Participles. (232—238.)

			The root and
Present & Future.	ಮಾಡುವ *máḍuva*,	who or which does, or will do.	ಉವ *uva*.
Past.	ಮಾಡಿದ *máḍida*, who or which did.		ಇದ *ida*.
Negative.	ಮಾಡದ *máḍada*,	who or which does not, did not, or will not do.	ಅದ *ada*.

Compound Relative Participles.

			The *present* gerund and
Present & Future.	ಮಾಡುತ್ತಿರುವ *máḍuttiruva*,	who or which is, or will be doing.	ಇರುವ *iruva*.†
Past.	ಮಾಡುತ್ತಿದ್ದ *máḍuttidda*,	who or which was doing.	ಇದ್ದ *idda*.‡
			The *past* gerund and
Perfect & Fut. perf.	ಮಾಡಿರುವ *máḍiruva*,	who or which has done, or will have done.	ಇರುವ *iruva*.
Pluperfect.	ಮಾಡಿದ್ದ *máḍidda*,	who or which had done.	ಇದ್ದ *idda*.

INFINITIVE MOOD. (239—246.)

		The root and
ಮಾಡ *máḍa*,	to do.	ಅ *a*.
ಮಾಡಲು *máḍalu*,		ಅಲು *alu*.
ಮಾಡಲಿಕ್ಕೆ *máḍalikke*,		ಅಲಿಕ್ಕೆ *alikke*.

---

* In the 2nd conjugation the affix is ಡು *du*.

† ಇರುವ *iruva*, who or which is, or will be, is the present and future relative participle of the verb ಇರು *iru*, Be. See its conjugation, (119.)

‡ ಇದ್ದ *idda*, who or which was, is the past relative participle of the same verb.

IMPERATIVE MOOD. (247—252.)

(Root and personal affixes.)

	SINGULAR.	PLURAL.
1st per.	ಮಾಡಲಿ *máḍali*, let me do.	ಮಾಡಲಿ *máḍali*, let us do.
2nd	ಮಾಡು * *máḍu*, do thou.	ಮಾಡಿರಿ *máḍiri*, do ye.
3rd mas. 3rd fem. 3rd neut.	ಮಾಡಲಿ *máḍali*, let him, her or it do.	ಮಾಡಲಿ *máḍali*, let them do.

NEGATIVE MOOD. (253.)

(Root and personal affixes.)

I, &c. do not, will not do, had not done, or would not have done.

1st per.	ಮಾಡೆನು *máḍenu*, I, &c.	ಮಾಡೆವು *máḍevu*, we, &c.
2nd.	ಮಾಡೆ *máḍe*, thou, &c.	ಮಾಡರಿ *máḍari*, ye, &c.
3rd mas.	ಮಾಡನು *máḍanu*, he, &c.	ಮಾಡರು *máḍaru*, they, &c.
3rd fem.	ಮಾಡಳು *máḍaḷu*, she, &c.	ಮಾಡರು *máḍaru*, ,,
3rd neut.	ಮಾಡದು *máḍadu*, it, &c.	ಮಾಡವು *máḍavu*, ,,

AFFIRMATIVE MOOD. (261—264.) SIMPLE TENSES.

PRESENT TENSE. I do, &c.

(Present Gerund ಮಾಡುತ್ತಾ *máḍuttá*, and personal affixes.)

1st per.	ಮಾಡುತ್ತೇನೆ *máḍutténe*, I do.	ಮಾಡುತ್ತೇವೆ *máḍuttéve*, we do.
2nd.	ಮಾಡುತ್ತೀ *máḍuttí*, thou, &c. or ಮಾಡುತ್ತೀಯೇ *máḍuttíyé*, ,,	ಮಾಡುತ್ತೀರಿ *máḍuttíri*, ye do.
3rd m.	ಮಾಡುತ್ತಾನೆ *máḍuttáne*, he, &c.	ಮಾಡುತ್ತಾರೆ *máḍuttáre*, they do.
3rd f.	ಮಾಡುತ್ತಾಳೆ *máḍuttáḷe*, she, &c.	ಮಾಡುತ್ತಾರೆ *máḍuttáre*, ,,
3rd n.	ಮಾಡುತ್ತದೆ *máḍuttade*, it, &c.	ಮಾಡುತ್ತವೆ *máḍuttave*, ,,

PAST TENSE. I did, &c.

(Past relative participle ಮಾಡಿದ *máḍida*, and personal affixes.)

1st per.	ಮಾಡಿದೆನು *máḍidenu*, I did.	ಮಾಡಿದೆವು *máḍidevu*, we did.
2nd.	ಮಾಡಿದಿ *máḍidi*, thou didst. or ಮಾಡಿದೆ *máḍide*, ,,	ಮಾಡಿದಿರಿ *máḍidiri*, ye did.

---

* The 2nd per. sing. Imperative is the root of the verb.

	SINGULAR.	PLURAL.
3rd m.	ಮಾಡಿದನು *máḍidanu*, he did.	ಮಾಡಿದರು *máḍidaru*, they did.
3rd f.	ಮಾಡಿದಳು *máḍidaḷu*, she did.	ಮಾಡಿದರು *máḍidaru*, ,,
3rd n.	ಮಾಡಿತು *máḍitu*, it did.	ಮಾಡಿದವು *máḍidavu*, ,,

1st FUTURE TENSE. I shall or will do, &c.

(Future relative participle ಮಾಡುವ *máḍuva*, and personal affixes.)

1st per.	ಮಾಡುವೆನು *máḍuvenu*, I, &c.	ಮಾಡುವೆವು *máḍuvevu*, we, &c.
2nd.	ಮಾಡುವಿ *máḍuvi*, thou, &c. or ಮಾಡುವೆ *máḍuve*, ,,	ಮಾಡುವಿರಿ *máḍuviri*, ye, &c.
3rd m.	ಮಾಡುವನು *máḍuvanu*, he, &c.	ಮಾಡುವರು *máḍuvaru*, they, &c.
3rd f.	ಮಾಡುವಳು *máḍuvaḷu*, she, &c.	ಮಾಡುವರು *máḍuvaru*, ,,
3rd n.	ಮಾಡುವದು *máḍuvadu*, it, &c.	ಮಾಡುವವು *máḍuvavu*, ,,

2nd or CONTINGENT FUTURE TENSE. I shall perhaps, or, I may do.

(Past gerund ಮಾಡಿ *máḍi*, and personal affixes.)

1st per.	ಮಾಡಿಯೇನು *máḍiyénu*, I, &c.	ಮಾಡಿಯೇವು *máḍiyévu*, we, &c.
2nd.	ಮಾಡೀಯೇ *máḍíyé*, thou, &c.	ಮಾಡೀರಿ *máḍíri*, ye, &c.
3rd m.	ಮಾಡಿಯಾನು *máḍiyánu*, he, &c.	ಮಾಡಿಯಾರು *máḍiyáru*, they, &c.
3rd f.	ಮಾಡಿಯಾಳು *máḍiyáḷu*, she, &c.	ಮಾಡಿಯಾರು *máḍiyáru*, ,,
3rd n.	ಮಾಡೀತು *máḍítu*, it, &c.	ಮಾಡಿಯಾವು *máḍiyávu*, ,,

COMPOUND TENSES.

There are six Compound Tenses in the Affirmative Mood; three are formed by adding to the *Present* Gerund of any verb, the present, past and future tenses of the verb ಇರು *iru*, Be. And three others are formed by adding the same tenses to the *Past* Gerund.

PRESENT TENSE. I am doing, &c.

(Present gerund ಮಾಡುತ್ತಾ *máḍuttá*, and the present tense of ಇರು *iru*.)

ಮಾಡುತ್ತಾಯಿದ್ಧೇನೆ *máḍuttá-iddhéne*,	ಮಾಡುತ್ತಾಯಿದ್ಧೇವೆ *máḍuttá-iddhéve*,
ಮಾಡುತ್ತಿದ್ಧೇನೆ *máḍuttiddhéne*, &c. &c.	ಮಾಡುತ್ತಿದ್ಧೇವೆ *máḍuttiddhéve*, &c. &c.

PAST TENSE. I was, or would have been, doing, &c.

(Present gerund ಮಾಡುತ್ತಾ *máḍuttá*, and the past tense of ಇರು *iru*.)

ಮಾಡುತ್ತಾಯಿದ್ದೆನು *máḍuttá-iddenu*,	ಮಾಡುತ್ತಾಯಿದ್ದೆವು *máḍuttá-iddevu*,
ಮಾಡುತ್ತಿದ್ದೆನು *máḍuttiddenu*, &c. &c.	ಮಾಡುತ್ತಿದ್ದೆವು *máḍuttiddevu*, &c. &c.

FUTURE TENSE. I shall or will be doing, &c.

(Present gerund ಮಾಡುತ್ತಾ *máḍuttá,* and the future tense of ಇರು *iru.*)

SINGULAR.	PLURAL.
ಮಾಡುತ್ತಾಯಿರುವೆನು *máḍuttá-iruvenu,*	ಮಾಡುತ್ತಾಯಿರುವೆವು *máḍuttá-iruvevu,*
ಮಾಡುತ್ತಿರುವೆನು *máḍuttiruvenu,* &c. &c.	ಮಾಡುತ್ತಿರುವೆವು *máḍuttiruvevu,* &c. &c.

PERFECT TENSE. I have done, &c.

(Past gerund ಮಾಡಿ *máḍi,* and present tense of ಇರು *iru.*)

ಮಾಡಿಯಿದ್ಧೇನೆ *máḍi-iddhéne,*	ಮಾಡಿಯಿದ್ಧೇವೆ *máḍi-iddhéve,*
ಮಾಡಿದ್ಧೇನೆ *máḍiddhéne,* &c. &c.	ಮಾಡಿದ್ಧೇವೆ *máḍiddhéve,* &c. &c.

PLUPERFECT TENSE. I had done, &c.

(Past gerund ಮಾಡಿ *máḍi,* and past tense of ಇರು *iru.*)

ಮಾಡಿಯಿದ್ದೆನು *máḍi-iddenu,*	ಮಾಡಿಯಿದ್ದೆವು *máḍi-iddevu,*
ಮಾಡಿದ್ದೆನು *máḍiddenu,* &c. &c.	ಮಾಡಿದ್ದೆವು *máḍiddevu,* &c. &c.

FUTURE PERFECT TENSE. I shall or will, or would have done, &c.

(Past gerund ಮಾಡಿ *máḍi,* and future tense of ಇರು *iru.*)

ಮಾಡಿಯಿರುವೆನು *máḍi-iruvenu,*	ಮಾಡಿಯಿರುವೆವು *máḍi-iruvevu,*
ಮಾಡಿರುವೆನು *máḍiruvenu,* &c. &c.	ಮಾಡಿರುವೆವು *máḍiruvevu,* &c. &c.

POTENTIAL MOOD. (265, 266.)

The Potential mood is formed by adding certain Auxiliary verbs to a principal verb in the Infinitive mood.

AFFIRMATIVE. MAY.	NEGATIVE. MAY NOT.
(Infinitive in ಅ, and ಬಹುದು.)	(Infinitive in ಅ and ಬಾರದು.)
I, &c. may do; or, am at liberty to do.	I, &c. may not do; or, am not at liberty to do.
ಮಾಡ ಬಹುದು *máḍa-bahudu.*	ಮಾಡ ಬಾರದು *máḍa-báradu.*
(Infinitive in ಅ and ಕೂಡುವದು.)	(Infinitive in ಅ and ಕೂಡದು.)
I, &c. may, or, am at liberty to do.	I, &c. may not, or, am not at liberty to do.
ಮಾಡಕೂಡುವದು *máḍa-kúḍuvadu.*	ಮಾಡಕೂಡದು *máḍa-kúḍadu.*
MUST.	MUST NOT.
(Infinitive in ಅ and ಬೇಕು.)	(Infinitive in ಅ and ಬೇಡ.)
I, &c. must, or need to do.	I, &c. must not, or, need not do.
ಮಾಡಬೇಕು *máḍa-béku.*	ಮಾಡಬೇಡ *maḍa-béḍa.*

Ought.

(Infinitive in ಅ and ತಕ್ಕದ್ದು.)

I, &c. ought to do; or, it is proper for me to do.

ಮಾಡತಕ್ಕದ್ದು *máḍa-takkaddu.*

The negative is formed by ತಕ್ಕದ್ದಲ್ಲ *takkaddalla.*

Can.

(Infinitive in ಅ and ಬಲ್ಲೆನು, &c. *)

I, &c. can do; or, I know to do.

ಮಾಡಬಲ್ಲೆನು *máḍa-ballenu.*

(Infinitive in ಉ and ಆಪೆನು, &c.)

I, &c. can, or, am able to do.

ಮಾಡಲಾಪೆನು *máḍal-ápenu.*

Cannot.

(Infinitive in ಉ and ಅರಿಯೆನು, &c.)

I, &c. cannot, or know not to do.

ಮಾಡಲರಿಯೆನು *máḍul-ariyenu.*

(Infinitive in ಉ and ಆರೆನು, &c.)

I, &c. cannot, am not able to do.

ಮಾಡಲಾರೆನು *máḍal-árenu.*

SUBJUNCTIVE MOOD. (265, 266.)

Aorist Tense. Impersonal.

(Past rel. part. ಮಾಡಿದ *máḍida,* and the affixes ರೆ *re,* ರೂ *rú,* and ಆಗ್ಯೂ *ágyú.*)

ಮಾಡಿದರೆ *máḍidare,* If I, &c. do, shall or should do.

ಮಾಡಿದರೂ *máḍidarú,*
ಮಾಡಿದಾಗ್ಯೂ *máḍidágyú,* } Although I do, shall or should do, &c.

Present and Future Tense. Impersonal.

(Present and fut. rel. part. ಮಾಡುವ *máḍuva,* and ಹಾಗೆ *háge,* that, so that.)

ಮಾಡುವ ಹಾಗೆ *máḍuva-háge,* that I, &c. may or might do.

Negative Impersonal.

(Negative Relative participle ಮಾಡದ *máḍada,* and ಹಾಗೆ *háge,* that, so that.)

ಮಾಡದ ಹಾಗೆ *máḍada-háge,* that I, &c. may not, or might not do.

Subjunctive Compound Tenses,

Formed by adding the Subjunctive Aorist Tense of ಇರು *iru,* Be, to the Present, Past, and Negative Gerunds of the principal verb.

Present Tense. Impersonal.

(Present gerund ಮಾಡುತ್ತಾ *máḍuttá,* and ಇದ್ದರೆ *iddare.*)

ಮಾಡುತ್ತಾ ಇದ್ದರೆ *máḍuttá-iddare,*
ಮಾಡುತ್ತಿದ್ದರೆ *máḍuttiddare,* } If I, &c. am doing.

---

*This and the following auxiliary verbs take the personal affixes. See conjugation of defective verbs. (122—128.)

PERFECT TENSE. Impersonal.

(Past gerund ಮಾಡಿ *máḍi*, and ಇದ್ದರೆ *iddare.*)

ಮಾಡಿ ಇದ್ದರೆ *máḍi-iddare,*
ಮಾಡಿದ್ದರೆ *máḍiddare,* } If I, &c. have done.

NEGATIVE. Impersonal.

(Negative gerund ಮಾಡದೆ *máḍade,* and ಇದ್ದರೆ *iddare.*)

ಮಾಡದೆ ಇದ್ದರೆ *máḍade-iddare,*
ಮಾಡದಿದ್ದರೆ *máḍadiddare,* } If I, &c. do not, did not, or will not do.

---

111. 2nd CONJUGATION, or a verb ending in ಎ *e.*

Root ಕರೆ *kare,* Call.

GERUNDS, or verbal participles. (223—231.)

		The root, and
Present.	ಕರೆಯುತ್ತ *kareyutta,* calling.	ಉತ್ತ *utta.*
—	ಕರೆಯುತ್ತಾ *kareyuttá,* „	ಉತ್ತಾ *uttá.*
Past.	ಕರೆದು *karedu,* having called.	ದು *du,* *
Negative.	ಕರೆಯದೆ *kareyade,* not having called.	ಅದೆ *ade.*

RELATIVE PARTICIPLES. (232—238.)

			The root and
Present & Future.	ಕರೆಯುವ *kareyuva,*	who or which calls, or will call.	ಉವ *uva.*
Past.	ಕರೆದ *kareda,*	who or which called.	ದ *da.*
Negative.	ಕರೆಯದ *kareyada,*	who or which calls not, called not, or will not call.	ಅದ *ada.*

COMPOUND RELATIVE PARTICIPLES.

			Present Gerund, and
Present & Future.	ಕರೆಯುತ್ತಿರುವ *kareyuttiruva,*	who or which is, or will be calling.	ಇರುವ *iruva.*
Past.	ಕರೆಯುತ್ತಿದ್ದ *kareyuttidda,*	who or which was calling.	ಇದ್ದ *idda.*
			Past gerund, and
Perfect & Fut. perf.	ಕರೆದಿರುವ *karediruva,*	who or which has, or will have, called.	ಇರುವ *iruva.*
Pluperfect.	ಕರೆದಿದ್ದ *karedidda,*	who or which had called.	ಇದ್ದ *idda.*

* In the 1st Conjugation the affix is ಇ *i.*

INFINITIVE MOOD. (239—246.)

		The root and
ಕರೆಯ *kareya*,	to call.	ಅ *a*.
ಕರೆಯಲು *kareyalu*,		ಅಲು *alu*.
ಕರೆಯಲಿಕ್ಕೆ *kareyalikke*,		ಅಲಿಕ್ಕೆ *alikke*.

IMPERATIVE MOOD. (247—252.)

(Root and personal affixes.)

Let me, &c. Call.

	SINGULAR.	PLURAL.
1st per.	ಕರೆಯಲಿ *kareyali*, let me call.	ಕರೆಯಲಿ *kareyali*, let us call.
2nd.	ಕರೆ * *kare*, call thou.	ಕರೆಯಿರಿ *kareyiri*, call ye.
3rd mas. / 3rd fem. / 3rd neut.	ಕರೆಯಲಿ *kareyali*, let him, her, or it call.	ಕರೆಯಲಿ *kareyali*, let them call.

NEGATIVE MOOD. (253.)

(Root and personal affixes.)

I, &c. call not, will not call.

1st per.	ಕರೆಯೆನು *kareyenu*, I, &c.	ಕರೆಯೆವು *kareyevu*, we, &c.
2nd.	ಕರೆಯೆ *kareye*, thou, &c.	ಕರೆಯರಿ *kareyari*, ye, &c.
3rd mas.	ಕರೆಯನು *kareyanu*, he, &c.	ಕರೆಯರು *kareyaru*, they, &c.
3rd fem.	ಕರೆಯಳು *kareyaḷu*, she, &c.	ಕರೆಯರು *kareyaru*, ,,
3rd neut.	ಕರೆಯದು *kareyadu*, it, &c.	ಕರೆಯವು *kareyavu*, ,,

AFFIRMATIVE MOOD. (261—264.) SIMPLE TENSES.

PRESENT TENSE. I call, &c.

(Present Gerund ಕರೆಯುತ್ತ *kareyutta*, and personal affixes.)

1st per.	ಕರೆಯುತ್ತೇನೆ *kareyuttêne*, I call.	ಕರೆಯುತ್ತೇವೆ *kareyuttêve*, we call.
2nd.	ಕರೆಯುತ್ತೀ *kareyuttí*, thou, &c.	ಕರೆಯುತ್ತೀರಿ *kareyuttíri*, ye call.
	ಕರೆಯುತ್ತೀಯೇ *kareyuttíyé*, ,,	
3rd m.	ಕರೆಯುತ್ತಾನೆ *kareyuttáne*, he, &c.	ಕರೆಯುತ್ತಾರೆ *kareyuttáre*, they, &c.
3rd f.	ಕರೆಯುತ್ತಾಳೆ *kareyuttáḷe*, she, &c.	ಕರೆಯುತ್ತಾರೆ *kareyuttáre*, ,,
3rd n.	ಕರೆಯುತ್ತದೆ *kareyuttade*, it, &c.	ಕರೆಯುತ್ತವೆ *kareyuttave*, ,,

---

* The 2nd per. sing. Imperative is the root of the verb.

2nd CONJUGATION.

PAST TENSE. I called, &c.

(Past relative participle ಕರೆದ *kareda*, and personal affixes.)

	SINGULAR.	PLURAL.
1st per.	ಕರೆದೆನು *karedenu*, I called.	ಕರೆದೆವು *karedevu*, we called.
2nd.	ಕರೆದಿ *karedi*, thou, &c.	ಕರೆದಿರಿ *karediri*, ye called.
	ಕರೆದೆ *karede*, ,,	
3rd m.	ಕರೆದನು *karedanu*, he, &c.	ಕರೆದರು *karedaru*, they &c.
3rd f.	ಕರೆದಳು *karedaḷu*, she, &c.	ಕರೆದರು *karedaru*, ,,
3rd n.	ಕರೆಯಿತು *kareyitu*, it, &c.	ಕರೆದವು *karedavu*, ,,

1st FUTURE TENSE. I shall or will call, &c.

(Future relative participle ಕರೆಯುವ *kareyuva*, and personal affixes.)

1st per.	ಕರೆಯುವೆನು *kareyuvenu*, I, &c.	ಕರೆಯುವೆವು *kareyuvevu*, we, &c.
2nd.	ಕರೆಯುವಿ *kareyuvi*, thou, &c.	ಕರೆಯುವಿರಿ *kareyuviri*, ye, &c.
	ಕರೆಯುವೆ *kareyuve*, ,,	
3rd m.	ಕರೆಯುವನು *kareyuvanu*, he, &c.	ಕರೆಯುವರು *kareyuvaru*, they, &c.
3rd f.	ಕರೆಯುವಳು *kareyuvaḷu*, she, &c.	ಕರೆಯುವರು *kareyuvaru*, ,,
3rd n.	ಕರೆಯುವದು *kareyuvadu*, it, &c.	ಕರೆಯುವವು *kareyuvavu*, ,,

2nd or CONTINGENT FUTURE TENSE. I shall perhaps, or, I may call.

(Past gerund ಕರೆದು *karedu*, and personal affixes.)

1st per.	ಕರೆದೇನು *karedénu*, I, &c.	ಕರೆದೇವು *karedévu*, we, &c.
2nd.	ಕರೆದೀಯೇ *karedíyé*, thou, &c.	ಕರೆದೀರಿ *karedíri*, ye, &c.
3rd m.	ಕರೆದಾನು *karedánu*, he, &c.	ಕರೆದಾರು *karedáru*, they, &c.
3rd f.	ಕರೆದಾಳು *karedáḷu*, she, &c.	ಕರೆದಾರು *karedáru*, ,,
3rd n.	ಕರೆದೀತು *karedítu*, it, &c.	ಕರೆದಾವು *karedávu*, ,,

COMPOUND TENSES.

There are six Compound Tenses in the Affirmative Mood. (See note in the 1st Conjugation.)

PRESENT TENSE. I am calling, &c.

(Present gerund ಕರೆಯುತ್ತಾ *kareyuttá*, and the present tense of ಇರು *iru*.)

ಕರೆಯುತ್ತಾಯಿದ್ಧೇನೆ *kareyuttá-iddhéne*, ಕರೆಯುತ್ತಾಯಿದ್ಧೇವೆ *kareyuttá-iddhéve*, ಕರೆಯುತ್ತಿದ್ಧೇನೆ *kareyuttiddhéne*, &c. &c. ಕರೆಯುತ್ತಿದ್ಧೇವೆ *kareyuttiddhéve*, &c. &c.

Past Tense. I was calling, &c.

(Present gerund ಕರೆಯುತ್ತಾ *kareyuttá*, and the past tense of ಇರು *iru.*)

Singular.	Plural.
ಕರೆಯುತ್ತಾಯಿದ್ದೆನು *kareyuttá-iddenu,*	ಕರೆಯುತ್ತಾಯಿದ್ದೆವು *kareyuttá-iddevu,*
ಕರೆಯುತ್ತಿದ್ದೆನು *kareyuttiddenu,* &c. &c.	ಕರೆಯುತ್ತಿದ್ದೆವು *kareyuttiddevu,* &c. &c.

Future Tense. I shall or will be calling, &c.

(Present gerund ಕರೆಯುತ್ತಾ *kareyuttá,* and the future tense of ಇರು *iru.*)

ಕರೆಯುತ್ತಾಯಿರುವೆನು *kareyuttá-iruvenu,*	ಕರೆಯುತ್ತಾಯಿರುವೆವು *kareyuttá-iruvevu,*
ಕರೆಯುತ್ತಿರುವೆನು *kareyuttiruvenu,* &c.	ಕರೆಯುತ್ತಿರುವೆವು *kareyuttiruvevu,* &c.

Perfect Tense. I have called, &c.

(Past gerund ಕರೆದು *karedu,* and present tense of ಇರು *iru.*)

ಕರೆದುಯಿದ್ಧೇನೆ *karedu-iddhéne,*	ಕರೆದುಯಿದ್ಧೇವೆ *karedu-iddhéve,*
ಕರೆದಿದ್ಧೇನೆ *karediddhéne,* &c. &c.	ಕರೆದಿದ್ಧೇವೆ *karediddhéve,* &c. &c.

Pluperfect Tense. I had called, &c.

(Past gerund ಕರೆದು *karedu,* and past tense of ಇರು *iru.*)

ಕರೆದುಯಿದ್ದೆನು *karedu-iddenu,*	ಕರೆದುಯಿದ್ದೆವು *karedu-iddevu,*
ಕರೆದಿದ್ದೆನು *karediddenu,* &c. &c.	ಕರೆದಿದ್ದೆವು *karediddevu,* &c. &c.

Future Perfect Tense. I shall or will, or would have called, &c.

(Past gerund ಕರೆದು *karedu,* and future tense of ಇರು *iru.*)

ಕರೆದುಯಿರುವೆನು *karedu-iruvenu,*	ಕರೆದುಯಿರುವೆವು *karedu-iruvevu,*
ಕರೆದಿರುವೆನು *karediruvenu,* &c. &c.	ಕರೆದಿರುವೆವು *karediruvevu,* &c. &c.

POTENTIAL MOOD. (265, 266.)

(See notes in the 1st Conjugation.)

Affirmative. May.	Negative. May not.
(Infinitive in ಅ, and ಬಹುದು.)	(Infinitive in ಅ and ಬಾರದು.)
I, &c. may call; or, am at liberty to call.	I, &c. may not call; or, am not at liberty to call.
ಕರೆಯ ಬಹುದು *kareya-bahudu.*	ಕರೆಯ ಬಾರದು *kareya-báradu.*
(Infinitive in ಅ and ಕೂಡುವದು.)	(Infinitive in ಅ and ಕೂಡದು.)
I, &c. may, or, am at liberty to call.	I, &c. may not, or, am not at liberty to call.
ಕರೆಯಕೂಡುವದು *kareya-kúḍuvadu.*	ಕರೆಯಕೂಡದು *kareya-kúḍadu.*

MUST.
(Infinitive in ಅ and ಬೇಕು.)
I, &c. must, or need to call.
ಕರೆಯಬೇಕು *kareya-béku.*

MUST NOT.
(Infinitive in ಅ and ಬೇಡ.)
I, &c. must not, or, need not call.
ಕರೆಯಬೇಡ *kareya-béda.*

OUGHT.
(Infinitive in ಅ and ತಕ್ಕದ್ದು.)
I, &c. ought to call; or, it is proper for me to call.
ಕರೆಯತಕ್ಕದ್ದು *kareya-takkaddu.*

The negative is formed by ತಕ್ಕದ್ದಲ್ಲ *takkaddalla.*

CAN.
(Infinitive in ಅ and ಬಲ್ಲ.)
I, &c. can call; or, I know to call.
ಕರೆಯಬಲ್ಲೆನು *kareya-ballenu.*

CANNOT.
(Infinitive in ಉ and ಅರಿಯನು.)
I, &c. cannot, or, know not to, call.
ಕರೆಯಲರಿಯೆನು *kareyal-ariyenu.*

(Infinitive in ಉ and ಆಪನು.)
I, &c. can call; or, I am able to call.
ಕರೆಯಲಾಪೆನು *kareyal-ápenu.*

(Infinitive in ಉ and ಆರನು.)
I, &c. cannot, or, am not able to, call.
ಕರೆಯಲಾರೆನು *kareyal-árenu.*

SUBJUNCTIVE MOOD. (265, 266.)

AORIST TENSE. Impersonal.

(Past rel. part. ಕರೆದ *kareda,* and the affixes ರೆ *re,* ರೂ *rú,* and ಆಗ್ಯೂ *ágyú.*)

ಕರೆದರೆ *karedare,* If I, &c. call, shall or should call.

ಕರೆದರೂ *karedarú,* }
ಕರೆದಾಗ್ಯೂ *karedágyú,* } Although I call, &c. &c.

PRESENT AND FUTURE TENSE. Impersonal.

(Pres. and fut. rel. part. ಕರೆಯುವ *kareyuva,* and ಹಾಗೆ *háge,* that, so that.)

ಕರೆಯುವಹಾಗೆ *kareyuva-háge,* that I, &c. may call.

NEGATIVE. Impersonal.

(Negative Rel. part. ಕರೆಯದ *kareyada,* and ಹಾಗೆ *háge,* that, so that.)

ಕರೆಯದಹಾಗೆ *kareyada-háge,* that I, &c. may *not* call.

COMPOUND TENSES.

Formed by adding the Subjunctive Aorist Tense of ಇರು *iru,* Be, to the Present, Past, and Negative Gerunds of the principal verb.

PRESENT TENSE. Impersonal.

(Present gerund ಕರೆಯುತ್ತಾ *kareyuttá,* and ಇದ್ದರೆ *iddare.*)

ಕರೆಯುತ್ತಾಇದ್ದರೆ *kareyuttá-iddare,* }
ಕರೆಯುತ್ತಿದ್ದರೆ *kareyuttiddare,* } If I, &c. am calling.

Perfect Tense. Impersonal.

(Past gerund ಕರೆದು *karedu*, and ಇದ್ದರೆ *iddare*.)

ಕರೆದುಇದ್ದರೆ *karedu-iddare*, ಕರೆದಿದ್ದರೆ *karediddare*,	If I, &c. have or had called.

Negative. Impersonal.

(Negative gerund ಕರೆಯದೆ *kareyade*, and ಇದ್ದರೆ *iddare*.)

ಕರೆಯದೆಇದ್ದರೆ *kareyade-iddare*, ಕರೆಯದಿದ್ದರೆ *kareyadiddare*,	If I, &c. call not, called not, or shall not call.

CAUSAL VERBS. (267.)

112. Causal verbs are formed by adding the affix ಇಸು *isu*, to the root of any verb of pure Canarese origin; as ಮಾಡಿಸು *máḍisu*, cause to do; ಕರೆಯಿಸು *kareyisu*, cause to call. The verbs so formed are conjugated like any regular verb ending in ಉ *u*; as in the following example.

(113.) Root ಮಾಡಿಸು *máḍisu*, Cause to do.

Gerunds.

			Compounded of the root and
Present.	ಮಾಡಿಸುತ್ತ *máḍisutta*, or ಮಾಡಿಸುತ್ತಾ *máḍisuttá*,	Causing to do.	ಉತ್ತ *utta*. ಉತ್ತಾ *uttá*.
Past.	ಮಾಡಿಸಿ *máḍisi*, having caused to do.		ಇ *i*,
Negative.	ಮಾಡಿಸದೆ *máḍisade*, not having caused to do.		ಅದೆ *ade*.

Relative Participles.

			The root and
Present & Future.	ಮಾಡಿಸುವ *máḍisuva*,	who or which causes, or will cause, to do.	ಉವ *uva*.
Past.	ಮಾಡಿಸಿದ *máḍisida*, who or which caused to do.		ಇದ *ida*.
Negative.	ಮಾಡಿಸದ *máḍisada*,	who or which does not, did not, or will not cause to do.	ಅದ *ada*.

Compound Relative Participles.

			The *present* gerund and
Present & Future.	ಮಾಡಿಸುತ್ತಿರುವ *máḍisuttiruva*,	who or which is, or will be, causing to do.	ಇರುವ *iruva*.
Past.	ಮಾಡಿಸುತ್ತಿದ್ದ *máḍisuttidda*,	who or which was causing to do.	ಇದ್ದ *idda*.
			The *past* gerund and
Perfect & Fut. perf.	ಮಾಡಿಸಿರುವ *máḍisiruva*,	who or which has, or will have, caused to do.	ಇರುವ *iruva*.
Pluperfect.	ಮಾಡಿಸಿದ್ದ *máḍisidda*,	who or which had caused to do.	ಇದ್ದ *idda*.

INFINITIVE MOOD.

		The root and
ಮಾಡಿಸ *máḍisa*,	to cause to do.	ಅ *a*.
ಮಾಡಿಸಲು *máḍisalu*,		ಅಲು *alu*.
ಮಾಡಿಸಲಿಕ್ಕೆ *máḍisalikke*,		ಅಲಿಕ್ಕೆ *alikke*.

IMPERATIVE MOOD. Let me, &c. cause to do.

(Root and personal affixes.)

	SINGULAR.	PLURAL.
1st per.	ಮಾಡಿಸಲಿ *máḍisali*.	ಮಾಡಿಸಲಿ *máḍisali*.
2nd.	ಮಾಡಿಸು *máḍisu*.	ಮಾಡಿಸಿರಿ *máḍisiri*.
3rd.	ಮಾಡಿಸಲಿ *máḍisali*.	ಮಾಡಿಸಲಿ *máḍisali*.

NEGATIVE MOOD. I, &c. do not or will not, cause to do.

(Root and personal affixes.)

ಮಾಡಿಸೆನು *máḍisenu*. ಮಾಡಿಸೆವು *máḍisevu*.

AFFIRMATIVE MOOD. *

PRESENT TENSE. I, &c. cause to do.

(Present gerund ಮಾಡಿಸುತ್ತ *máḍisutta*, and personal affixes.)

ಮಾಡಿಸುತ್ತೇನೆ *máḍisutténe*, &c. &c. ಮಾಡಿಸುತ್ತೇವೆ *máḍisuttéve*, &c. &c.

PAST TENSE. I, &c. caused to do.

(Past Relative participle ಮಾಡಿಸಿದ *máḍisida*, and personal affixes.)

ಮಾಡಿಸಿದೆನು *máḍisidenu*, &c. &c. ಮಾಡಿಸಿದೆವು *máḍisidevu*, &c. &c.

1st FUTURE TENSE. I, &c. shall or will cause to do.

(Future Relative participle ಮಾಡಿಸುವ *máḍisuva*, and personal affixes.)

ಮಾಡಿಸುವೆನು *máḍisuvenu*, &c. &c. ಮಾಡಿಸುವೆವು *máḍisuvevu*, &c. &c.

2nd or CONTINGENT FUTURE. I shall perhaps cause to do.

(Past gerund ಮಾಡಿಸಿ *máḍisi*, and personal affixes.)

ಮಾಡಿಸಿಯೇನು *máḍisiyénu*, &c. &c. ಮಾಡಿಸಿಯೇವು *máḍisiyévu*, &c. &c.

* The compound tenses of this mood, as well as the potential and subjunctive moods, are formed like any other regular verb of the 1st conjugation.

PASSIVE VERBS. (268.)

114. Any active verb may be made passive by cutting off the final vowel of the Infinitive in ಲು *lu*, and adding the irregular verb ಪಡು *paḍu*, experience, enjoy, suffer, &c., throughout all its moods, tenses, &c. The passive form of verbs is comparatively rarely used.

Root, ಕರೆಯಲ್ಪಡು *kareyalpaḍu*, (ಕರೆಯಲು *kareyalu*, and ಪಡು *paḍu*,) Be Called.

Gerunds.

		The root, and
Present.	ಕರೆಯಲ್ಪಡುತ್ತ *kareyalpaḍutta*, being called.	ಉತ್ತ *utta*.
	ಕರೆಯಲ್ಪಡುತ್ತಾ *kareyalpaḍuttá*, „	ಉತ್ತಾ *uttá*.
Past.	ಕರೆಯಲ್ಪಟ್ಟು* *kareyalpaṭṭu*, having been called.	Irregular.
Negative.	ಕರೆಯಲ್ಪಡದೆ *kareyalpaḍade*, not having been called.	ಅದೆ *ade*.

Relative Participles.

			The root and
Present & Future.	ಕರೆಯಲ್ಪಡುವ *kareyalpaḍuva*,	who or which is, or will be, called.	ಉವ *uva*.
Past.	ಕರೆಯಲ್ಪಟ್ಟ *kareyalpaṭṭa*,	who or which was called.	Irregular.
Negative.	ಕರೆಯಲ್ಪಡದ *kareyalpaḍada*,	who or which is not, was not, or will not, be called.	ಅದ *ada*.

Compound Relative Participles.

			Present Gerund, and
Pres. & Future.	ಕರೆಯಲ್ಪಡುತ್ತಿರುವ *kareyalpaḍuttiruva*,	who or which is being called.	ಇರುವ *iruva*.
Past.	ಕರೆಯಲ್ಪಡುತ್ತಿದ್ದ *kareyalpaḍuttidda*,	who or which was being called.	ಇದ್ದ *idda*.
			Past gerund, and
Perfect & Fut. perf.	ಕರೆಯಲ್ಪಟ್ಟಿರುವ *kareyalpaṭṭiruva*,	who or which has or will have, been called.	ಇರುವ *iruva*.
Pluperfect.	ಕರೆಯಲ್ಪಟ್ಟಿದ್ದ *kareyalpaṭṭidda*,	who or which had been called.	ಇದ್ದ *idda*.

INFINITIVE MOOD.

		The root, and
ಕರೆಯಲ್ಪಡ *kareyalpaḍa*,	to be called.	ಅ *a*.
ಕರೆಯಲ್ಪಡಲು *kareyalpaḍalu*,		ಅಲು *alu*.
ಕರೆಯಲ್ಪಡಲಿಕ್ಕೆ *kareyalpaḍalikke*,		ಅಲಿಕ್ಕೆ *alikke*.

---

* Whenever the past gerund is irregular, or ends in ಉ *u*, the past relative participle is formed from it by changing the final ಉ *u*, into ಅ *a*.

IMPERATIVE MOOD. Let me, &c. be called.

(Root and personal affixes.)

	Singular.	Plural.
1st per.	ಕರೆಯಲ್ಪಡಲಿ *kareyalpaḍali.*	ಕರೆಯಲ್ಪಡಲಿ *kareyalpaḍali.*
2nd.	ಕರೆಯಲ್ಪಡು *kareyalpaḍu.*	ಕರೆಯಲ್ಪಡಿರಿ *kareyalpaḍiri.*
3rd.	ಕರೆಯಲ್ಪಡಲಿ *kareyalpaḍali.*	ಕರೆಯಲ್ಪಡಲಿ *kareyalpaḍali.*

NEGATIVE MOOD. I, &c. am not, or shall not, be called.

(Root and personal affixes.)

Singular.	Plural.
ಕರೆಯಲ್ಪಡೆನು *kareyalpaḍenu*, &c.	ಕರೆಯಲ್ಪಡೆವು *kareyalpaḍevu*, &c.

AFFIRMATIVE MOOD.

Present Tense. I, &c. am called.

(Present gerund ಕರೆಯಲ್ಪಡುತ್ತ *kareyalpaḍutta*, and personal affixes.)

ಕರೆಯಲ್ಪಡುತ್ತೇನೆ *kareyalpaḍutténe*, &c. &c. — ಕರೆಯಲ್ಪಡುತ್ತೇವೆ *kareyalpaḍuttéve*, &c. &c.

Past Tense. I, &c. was called.

(Past rel. part. ಕರೆಯಲ್ಪಟ್ಟ *kareyalpaṭṭa*, and personal affixes.)

ಕರೆಯಲ್ಪಟ್ಟೆನು *kareyalpaṭṭenu*, &c. &c. — ಕರೆಯಲ್ಪಟ್ಟೆವು *kareyalpaṭṭevu*, &c. &c.

1st. Future Tense. I, &c. shall or will be called.

(Future rel. part. ಕರೆಯಲ್ಪಡುವ *kareyalpaḍuva*, and personal affixes.)

ಕರೆಯಲ್ಪಡುವೆನು *kareyalpaḍuvenu*, &c. &c. — ಕರೆಯಲ್ಪಡುವೆವು *kareyalpaḍuvevu*, &c. &c.

2nd or Contingent Future. I, &c. shall perhaps be called.

(Past gerund ಕರೆಯಲ್ಪಟ್ಟು *kareyalpaṭṭu*, and personal affixes).

ಕರೆಯಲ್ಪಟ್ಟೇನು *kareyalpaṭṭénu*, &c. &c. — ಕರೆಯಲ್ಪಟ್ಟೇವು *kareyalpaṭṭévu*, &c. &c.

Compound Tenses.

Present Tense. I am being called; literally, being called, I am.

(Present gerund ಕರೆಯಲ್ಪಡುತ್ತಾ *kareyalpaḍutta*, and pres. tense of ಇರು *iru.*)

Sing. ಕರೆಯಲ್ಪಡುತ್ತಾಯಿದ್ದೇನೆ *kareyalpaḍuttá-iddhéne.*

PAST TENSE. I was being called; *lit.* Being called, I was.

(Present gerund as above, and the past tense of ಇರು *iru.*)

ಕರೆಯಲ್ಪಡುತ್ತಾಯಿದ್ದೆನು *kareyalpaḍuttá-iddenu.*

FUTURE TENSE. I shall or will be being called; *lit.* Being called, I shall or will be.

(Present gerund as above, and the future tense of ಇರು *iru.*)

ಕರೆಯಲ್ಪಡುತ್ತಾಯಿರುವೆನು *kareyalpaḍuttá-iruvenu.*

PERFECT TENSE. I have been called; *lit.* Having been called, I am.

(Past gerund ಕರೆಯಲ್ಪಟ್ಟು *kareyalpaṭṭu,* and present tense of ಇರು *iru.*)

ಕರೆಯಲ್ಪಟ್ಟುಯಿದ್ಧೇನೆ *kareyalpaṭṭu-iddhéne.*

PLUPERFECT TENSE. I had been called; *lit.* Having been called, I was.

(Past gerund as above, and past tense of ಇರು *iru.*)

ಕರೆಯಲ್ಪಟ್ಟುಯಿದ್ದೆನು *kareyalpaṭṭu-iddenu.*

FUTURE PERFECT TENSE. I shall or will have been called; *lit.* Having been called, I shall or will be.

(Past gerund as above, and future tense of ಇರು *iru.*)

ಕರೆಯಲ್ಪಟ್ಟುಯಿರುವೆನು *kareyalpaṭṭu-iruvenu.*

POTENTIAL MOOD.

(See notes in the 1st Conjugation.)

AFFIRMATIVE. MAY.
(Infinitive in ಅ, and ಬಹುದು.)

I, &c. may be called.
ಕರೆಯಲ್ಪಡಬಹುದು *kareyalpaḍa-bahudu.*

NEGATIVE. MAY NOT.
(Infinitive in ಅ and ಬಾರದು.)

I, &c. may not be called.
ಕರೆಯಲ್ಪಡಬಾರದು *kareyalpaḍa-bárudu.*

(Infinitive in ಅ and ಕೂಡುವದು.)

I, &c. may be called.
ಕರೆಯಲ್ಪಡಕೂಡುವದು *kareyalpaḍa-kúḍuvadu.*

(Infinitive in ಅ and ಕೂಡದು.)

I, &c. may not be called.
ಕರೆಯಲ್ಪಡಕೂಡದು *kareyalpaḍa-kúḍadu.*

MUST.
(Infinitive in ಅ and ಬೇಕು.)

I, &c. must be called.
ಕರೆಯಲ್ಪಡಬೇಕು *kareyalpaḍa-béku.*

MUST NOT.
(Infinitive in ಅ and ಬೇಡ.)

I, &c. must not be called.
ಕರೆಯಲ್ಪಡಬೇಡ *kareyalpaḍa-béḍa.*

PASSIVE VERBS.

OUGHT.

(Infinitive in ಅ and ತಕ್ಕದ್ದು.)

I, &c. ought to be called.

ಕರೆಯಲ್ಪಡತಕ್ಕದ್ದು *kareyalpaḍa-takkaddu.*

The negative is formed by ತಕ್ಕದ್ದಲ್ಲ *takkaddalla.*

CAN.

(Infinitive in ಅ and ಬಲ್ಲೆನು.)

I, &c. can be called.

ಕರೆಯಲ್ಪಡಬಲ್ಲೆನು *kareyalpaḍa-ballenu.*

(Infinitive in ಲು and ಆಪೆನು.)

I, &c. can be called.

ಕರೆಯಲ್ಪಡಲಾಪೆನು *kareyalpaḍal-ápenu.*

CANNOT.

(Infinitive in ಲು and ಅರಿಯೆನು.)

I, &c. cannot be called.

ಕರೆಯಲ್ಪಡಲರಿಯೆನು *kareyalpaḍal-ariyenu.*

(Infinitive in ಲು and ಆರೆನು.)

I, &c. cannot be called.

ಕರೆಯಲ್ಪಡಲಾರೆನು *kareyalpaḍal-árenu.*

SUBJUNCTIVE MOOD.

AORIST TENSE.

(Past rel. part. ಕರೆಯಲ್ಪಟ್ಟ *kareyalpaṭṭa,* and the affixes ರೆ *re,* ರೂ *rú,* and ಆಗ್ಯೂ *ágyú.*)

ಕರೆಯಲ್ಪಟ್ಟರೆ *kareyalpaṭṭare,* If I, &c. am called, was called, &c.

PRESENT AND FUTURE TENSE.

(Pres. and fut. rel. part. ಕರೆಯಲ್ಪಡುವ *kareyalpaḍuva,* and ಹಾಗೆ *háge,* so that, &c.)

ಕರೆಯಲ್ಪಡುವಹಾಗೆ *kareyalpaḍuva-háge,* that I, &c. may be called.

NEGATIVE.

(Neg. Rel. part. ಕರೆಯಲ್ಪಡದ *kareyalpaḍada,* and ಹಾಗೆ *háge,* so that, &c.)

ಕರೆಯಲ್ಪಡದಹಾಗೆ *kareyalpaḍada-háge,* that I, &c. may *not* call.

COMPOUND TENSES.

Formed by adding the Subjunctive Aorist Tense of ಇರು *iru,* Be, to the Present, Past, and Negative Gerunds of the principal verb.

PRESENT TENSE.

(Present gerund ಕರೆಯಲ್ಪಡುತ್ತಾ *kareyalpaḍuttá,* and ಇದ್ದರೆ *iddare.*)

ಕರೆಯಲ್ಪಡುತ್ತಿದ್ದರೆ *kareyalpaḍuttiddare,* If I, &c. am being called.

PERFECT TENSE.

(Past gerund ಕರೆಯಲ್ಪಟ್ಟು *kareyalpaṭṭu*, and ಇದ್ದರೆ *iddare*.)

ಕರೆಯಲ್ಪಟ್ಟಿದ್ದರೆ *kareyalpaṭṭiddare*, If I, &c. have been called.

NEGATIVE.

(Negative gerund ಕರೆಯಲ್ಪಡದೆ *kareyalpaḍade*, and ಇದ್ದರೆ *iddare*.)

ಕರೆಯಲ್ಪಡದಿದ್ದರೆ *kareyalpaḍadiddare*, If I, &c. am not, or was not, called, &c.

IRREGULAR VERBS.

115. About one hundred verbs are irregular in the Past Gerund; which affects the Past Participle, the Past tense, and the Contingent Future. In these verbs, the Past Gerund is formed by changing the final syllable of the root into ಟ್ಟು *ṭṭu*, ತು *tu*, ದು *du*, ಕು *ku*, &c. Whether the verb be of the First or Second conjugation, the irregular past gerund always ends in ಉ *u*, and the past participle is formed from it by changing ಉ *u*, into ಅ *a*. From these, the past tense and the contingent future are formed by cutting off the final vowels, and adding the personal affixes, according to rule. Thus,

The root of the verb	ಕೊಡು *koḍu*.
Past gerund	ಕೊಟ್ಟು *koṭṭu*.
Past participle	ಕೊಟ್ಟ *koṭṭa*.
Past Tense (1st per sing.)	ಕೊಟ್ಟೆನು *koṭṭenu*.
Contingent Future (1st per sing.)	ಕೊಟ್ಟೇನು *koṭṭénu*.

116. The 3rd per. sing. neut. past tense is also given in the following list to remove all difficulty respecting it, out of the learner's way. But the other personal affixes, being regular, as well as the past participle, are not given in the following tabular form.

LIST OF IRREGULAR VERBS.

	Past Gerund.	Past Tense. 1st per. sing.	Past Tense. 3rd per. sing. neut.	Con. Future. 1st per. sing.
ಅಡು *aḍu*, Cook.	ಅಟ್ಟು *aṭṭu*.	ಅಟ್ಟೆನು *aṭṭenu*.	ಅಟ್ಟಿತು *aṭṭitu*.	ಅಟ್ಟೇನು *aṭṭénu*.
ಅರಿ *ari*, Know.	ಅರಿತು *aritu*.	ಅರಿತೆನು *aritenu*.	ಅರಿಯಿತು *ariyitu*.	ಅರಿತೇನು *ariténu*.
ಅಲೆ *ale*, Wander.	ಅಲೆತು *aletu*.	ಅಲೆತೆನು *aletenu*.	ಅಲೆಯಿತು *aleyitu*.	ಅಲೆತೇನು *aleténu*.
	ಅಲೆದು *aledu*.	ಅಲೆದೆನು *aledenu*.		ಅಲೆದೇನು *aledénu*.
ಅವಿ *avi*, Conceal.	ಅವಿತು *avitu*.	ಅವಿತೆನು *avitenu*.	ಅವಿಯಿತು *aviyitu*.	ಅವಿತೇನು *aviténu*.
ಅಳು *aḷu*, Weep.	ಅತ್ತು *attu*.	ಅತ್ತೆನು *attenu*.	ಅತ್ತಿತು *attitu*.	ಅತ್ತೇನು *atténu*.
ಅನ್ನು *annu*, Say.	ಅಂದು *andu*.	ಅಂದೆನು *andenu*.	ಅಂದಿತು *anditu*.	ಅಂದೇನು *andénu*.
ಆಗು *águ*, Become.	ಆಗಿ *ági*.	ಆದೆನು *ádenu*.	ಆಯಿತು *áyitu*.	ಆದೇನು *ádénu*.
ಆನು *ánu*, Prop, recline.	ಆತು *átu*.	ಆತೆನು *átenu*.	ಆತಿತು *átitu*.	ಆತೇನು *áténu*.
ಆಸರು *ásaru*, Be tired.	ಆಸತ್ತು *ásattu*.	ಆಸತ್ತೆನು *ásattenu*.	ಆಸತ್ತಿತು *ásattitu*.	ಆಸತ್ತೇನು, *ásatténu*.
ಇಡು *iḍu*, Keep, put.	ಇಟ್ಟು *iṭṭu*.	ಇಟ್ಟೆನು *iṭṭenu*.	ಇಟ್ಟಿತು *iṭṭitu*.	ಇಟ್ಟೇನು *iṭṭénu*.
ಇರು *iru*, Be, exist.	ಇದ್ದು *iddu*.	ಇದ್ದೆನು *iddenu*.	ಇತ್ತು *ittu*.	ಇದ್ದೇನು *iddénu*.
ಈ *í*, (2 per. sing. Imp. ಈಯಿ *íyi*,) Give.	ಇತ್ತು *ittu*.	ಇತ್ತೆನು *ittenu*.	ಇತ್ತಿತು *ittitu*.	ಇತ್ತೇನು *itténu*.
ಈನು *ínu*, Yean, bring forth.	ಈದು *ídu*.		ಈಯಿತು *íyitu*.	
ಉಗು *ugu*, Throw.	ಉಕ್ಕು *ukku*.	ಉಕ್ಕೆನು *ukkenu*.	ಉಕ್ಕಿತು *ukkitu*.	ಉಕ್ಕೇನು *ukkénu*.
ಉಡು *uḍu*, Dress.	ಉಟ್ಟು *uṭṭu*.	ಉಟ್ಟೆನು *uṭṭenu*.	ಉಟ್ಟಿತು *uṭṭitu*.	ಉಟ್ಟೇನು *uṭṭénu*.
ಉಣ್ಣು *uṇṇu*, Eat.	ಉಂಡು *uṇḍu*.	ಉಂಡೆನು *uṇḍenu*.	ಉಂಡಿತು *uṇḍitu*.	ಉಂಡೇನು *uṇḍénu*.

		Past Tense.		Con. Future.
	Past Gerund.	1st per. sing.	3rd per. sing. neut.	1st per. sing.
ಉಳ್ಳು *uḷu*, Plough.	ಉತ್ತು *uttu*.	ಉತ್ತೆನು *uttenu*.	ಉತ್ತಿತು *uttitu*.	ಉತ್ತೇನು *utténu*.
ಎಚ್ಚರು *yechcharu*, Be watchful.	ಎಚ್ಚತ್ತು *yechchattu*.	ಎಚ್ಚತ್ತೆನು *yechchattenu*.	ಎಚ್ಚತ್ತಿತು *yechchattitu*.	ಎಚ್ಚತ್ತೇನು *yechchatténu*.
ಎನ್ನು *yennu*, Say.	ಎಂದು *yendu*.	ಎಂದೆನು *yendenu*.	ಎಂದಿತು *yenditu*.	ಎಂದೇನು *yendénu*.
ಎಸೆ *yese*, Shoot with an arrow.	ಎಸೆದು *yesedu*.	ಎಸೆದೆನು *yesedenu*.	ಎಸೆಯಿತು *yeseyitu*.	ಎಸೆದೇನು *yesedénu*.
	ಎಸೆತು *yesetu*.	ಎಸೆತೆನು *yesetenu*.		ಎಸೆತೇನು *yeseténu*.
ಏಳ್ಳು *yéḷu*, Arise.	ಎದ್ದು *yeddu*.	ಎದ್ದೆನು *yeddenu*.	ಎದ್ದಿತು *yedditu*.	ಎದ್ದೇನು *yeddénu*.
ಒದೆ *wode*, Kick.	ಒದ್ದು *woddu*.	ಒದ್ದೆನು *woddenu*.	ಒದ್ದಿತು *wodditu*.	ಒದ್ದೇನು *woddénu*.
ಕದಿ *kadi*, Steal.	ಕದ್ದು *kaddu*.	ಕದ್ದೆನು *kaddenu*.	ಕದಿಯಿತು *kadiyitu*.	ಕದ್ದೇನು *kaddénu*.
ಕಲಿ *kali*, Learn.	ಕಲಿತು *kalitu*.	ಕಲಿತೆನು *kalitenu*.	ಕಲಿಯಿತು *kaliyitu*.	ಕಲಿತೇನು *kaliténu*.
ಕವಲು *kavalu*, Separate into two branches.	ಕವಲ್ತು *kavaltu*.	ಕವಲ್ತೆನು *kavaltenu*.	ಕವಲಿತು *kavalitu*.	ಕವಲ್ತೇನು *kavalténu*.
ಕಳ್ಳಿ *kaḷi*, Löse.	ಕಳಿತು *kaḷitu*.	ಕಳಿತೆನು *kaḷitenu*.	ಕಳಿಯಿತು *kaḷiyitu*.	ಕಳಿತೇನು *kaḷiténu*.
ಕಳ್ಳು *kaḷu*, Steal.	ಕದ್ದು *kaddu*.	ಕದ್ದೆನು *kaddenu*.	ಕದ್ದಿತು *kadditu*.	ಕದ್ದೇನು *kaddénu*.
ಕಾ *ká*, (2nd per. Imp. ಕಾಯಿ *káyi*,) Protect.	ಕಾದು *kádu*.	ಕಾದೆನು *kádenu*.	ಕಾಯಿತು *káyitu*.	ಕಾದೇನು *kádénu*.
ಕಾಣು *káṇu*, See.	ಕಂಡು *kaṇḍu*.	ಕಂಡೆನು *kaṇḍenu*.	ಕಂಡಿತು *kaṇḍitu*.	ಕಂಡೇನು *kaṇḍénu*.
ಕಿಸಿ *kisi*, Grin.	ಕಿಸಿದು *kisidu*.	ಕಿಸಿದೆನು *kisidenu*.	ಕಿಸಿಯಿತು *kisiyitu*.	ಕಿಸಿದೇನು *kisidénu*.
	ಕಿಸಿತು *kisitu*.	ಕಿಸಿತೆನು *kisitenu*.		ಕಿಸಿತೇನು *kisiténu*.
ಕೀ *kí*, Become pus.	ಕೀತು *kítu*.		ಕೀಯಿತು *kíyitu*.	
ಕೀಳ್ಳು *kíḷu*, Pluck up.	ಕಿತ್ತು *kittu*.	ಕಿತ್ತೆನು *kittenu*.	ಕಿತ್ತಿತು *kittitu*.	ಕಿತ್ತೇನು *kitténu*.

		Past Tense.		Con. Future.
	Past Gerund.	1st per. sing.	3rd per. sing. neut.	1st per. sing.
ಕುರಿ *kuri*, Aim.	ಕುರಿತು *kuritu*.	ಕುರಿತೆನು *kuritenu*.	ಕುರಿಯಿತು *kuriyitu*.	ಕುರಿತೇನು *kuriténu*.
ಕುಸಿ *kusi*, Sink down.	ಕುಸಿದು *kusidu*.	ಕುಸಿದೆನು *kusidenu*.	ಕುಸಿಯಿತು *kusiyitu*.	ಕುಸಿದೇನು *kusidénu*.
	ಕುಸಿತು *kusitu*.	ಕುಸಿತೆನು *kusitenu*.		ಕುಸಿತೇನು *kusiténu*.
ಕೂರು *kúru*, Sit.	ಕೂತು *kútu*.	ಕೂತೆನು *kútenu*.	ಕೂತಿತು *kútitu*.	ಕೂತೇನು *kúténu*.
ಕೆಡು *keḍu*, Spoil.	ಕೆಟ್ಟು *keṭṭu*.	ಕೆಟ್ಟೆನು *keṭṭenu*.	ಕೆಟ್ಟಿತು *keṭṭitu*.	ಕೆಟ್ಟೇನು *keṭṭénu*.
ಕೊಡು *koḍu*, Give.	ಕೊಟ್ಟು *koṭṭu*.	ಕೊಟ್ಟೆನು *koṭṭenu*.	ಕೊಟ್ಟಿತು *koṭṭitu*.	ಕೊಟ್ಟೇನು *koṭṭénu*.
ಕೊನರು *konaru*, Sprout.	ಕೊನರ್ತು *konartu*.	ಕೊನರ್ತೆನು *konartenu*.	ಕೊನರಿತು *konaritu*.	ಕೊನರ್ತೇನು *konarténu*.
ಕೊಲ್ಲು *kollu*, Kill.	ಕೊಂದು *kondu*.	ಕೊಂದೆನು *kondenu*.	ಕೊಂದಿತು *konditu*.	ಕೊಂದೇನು *kondénu*.
ಕೊಳ್ಳು *koḷḷu*, Buy, take.	ಕೊಂಡು *koṇḍu*.	ಕೊಂಡೆನು *koṇḍenu*.	ಕೊಂಡಿತು *koṇḍitu*.	ಕೊಂಡೇನು *koṇḍénu*.
ಕೊಳೆ *koḷe*, Rot.	ಕೊಳೆತು *koḷetu*.	ಕೊಳೆತೆನು *koḷetenu*.	ಕೊಳೆಯಿತು *koḷeyitu*.	ಕೊಳೆತೇನು *koḷeténu*.
ಗೆಲ್ಲು *gellu*, Win.	ಗೆದ್ದು *geddu*.	ಗೆದ್ದೆನು *geddenu*.	ಗೆದ್ದಿತು *gedditu*.	ಗೆದ್ದೇನು *geddénu*.
ಗೋಳಿಡು *góḷiḍu*, Lament.	ಗೋಳಿಟ್ಟು *góḷiṭṭu*.	ಗೋಳಿಟ್ಟೆನು *góḷiṭṭenu*.	ಗೋಳಿಟ್ಟಿತು *góḷiṭṭitu*.	ಗೋಳಿಟ್ಟೇನು *góḷiṭṭénu*.
ಚಳಿ *chaḷi*, Be tired.	ಚಳಿತು *chaḷitu*.	ಚಳಿತೆನು *chaḷitenu*.	ಚಳಿಯಿತು *chaḷiyitu*.	ಚಳಿತೇನು *chaḷiténu*.
ಚಿಗುರು *chiguru*, Sprout.	ಚಿಗುರ್ತು *chigurtu*.	ಚಿಗುರ್ತೆನು *chigurtenu*.	ಚಿಗುರಿತು *chiguritu*.	ಚಿಗುರ್ತೇನು *chigurténu*.
ಜೋಲು *jólu*, Swing.	ಜೋತು *jótu*.	ಜೋತೆನು *jótenu*.	ಜೋತಿತು *jótitu*.	ಜೋತೇನು *jóténu*.
ತರು *taru*, Bring.	ತಂದು *tandu*.	ತಂದೆನು *tandenu*.	ತಂದಿತು *tanditu*.	ತಂದೇನು *tandénu*.
ತಳಿರು *taḷiru*, Sprout.	ತಳಿರ್ತು *taḷirtu*.	ತಳಿರ್ತೆನು *taḷirtenu*.	ತಳಿರಿತು *tuḷiritu*.	ತಳಿರ್ತೇನು *taḷirténu*.
ತಿನ್ನು *tinnu*, Eat.	ತಿಂದು *tindu*.	ತಿಂದೆನು *tindenu*.	ತಿಂದಿತು *tinditu*.	ತಿಂದೇನು *tindénu*.
ತೇ *té*, (2nd per. sing. imp. ತೇಯಿ *téyi*,) Grind, rub.	ತೇದು *tédu*.	ತೇದೆನು *tédenu*.	ತೇಯಿತು *téyitu*.	ತೇದೇನು *tédénu*.

	Past Gerund.	Past Tense. 1st per. sing.	Past Tense. 3rd per. sing. neut.	Con. Future. 1st per. sing.
ತೆರು *teru*, Pay taxes.	ತೆತ್ತು *tettu*.	ತೆತ್ತೆನು *tettenu*.	ತೆತ್ತಿತು *tettitu*.	ತೆತ್ತೇನು *tetténu*.
ತೊಡು *toḍu*, Dress, prepare.	ತೊಟ್ಟು *toṭṭu*.	ತೊಟ್ಟೆನು *toṭṭenu*.	ತೊಟ್ಟಿತು *toṭṭitu*.	ತೊಟ್ಟೇನು *toṭṭénu*.
ತೋ *tó*, Be wet.	ತೋಯಿದು *tóyidu*.	ತೋಯಿದೆನು *tóyidenu*.	ತೋಯಿತು *tóyitu*.	ತೋಯಿದೇನು *tóyidénu*.
ನಗು *nagu*, Laugh.	ನಕ್ಕು *nakku*.	ನಕ್ಕೆನು *nakkenu*.	ನಕ್ಕಿತು *nakkitu*.	ನಕ್ಕೇನು *nakkénu*.
ನಿಲ್ಲು *nillu*, Stop.	ನಿಂತು *nintu*.	ನಿಂತೆನು *nintenu*.	ನಿಂತಿತು *nintitu*.	ನಿಂತೇನು *ninténu*.
ನುಸಿ *nusi*, Creep.	ನುಸಿದು *nusidu*.	ನುಸಿದೆನು *nusidenu*.	ನುಸಿಯಿತು *nusiyitu*.	ನುಸಿದೇನು *nusidénu*.
	ನುಸಿತು *nusitu*.	ನುಸಿತೆನು *nusitenu*.		ನುಸಿತೇನು *nusiténu*.
ನೂಲು *núlu*, Spin.	ನೂತು *nútu*.	ನೂತೆನು *nútenu*.	ನೂತಿತು *nútitu*.	ನೂತೇನು *núténu*.
ನೆಡು *neḍu*, Plant.	ನೆಟ್ಟು *neṭṭu*.	ನೆಟ್ಟೆನು *neṭṭenu*.	ನೆಟ್ಟಿತು *neṭṭitu*.	ನೆಟ್ಟೇನು *neṭṭénu*.
ನೇಲು *nélu*, Swing.	ನೇತು *nétu*.	ನೇತೆನು *nétenu*.	ನೇತಿತು *nétitu*.	ನೇತೇನು *néténu*.
ನೋ *nó*, Be in pain.	ನೊಂದು *nondu*.	ನೊಂದೆನು *nondenu*.	ನೊಂದಿತು *nonditu*.	ನೊಂದೇನು *nondénu*.
ನೋನು *nónu*, Perform a vow.	ನೋತು *nótu*.	ನೋತೆನು *nótenu*.	ನೋತಿತು *nótitu*.	ನೋತೇನು *nóténu*.
ಪಡು *paḍu*, Experience.	ಪಟ್ಟು *paṭṭu*.	ಪಟ್ಟೆನು *paṭṭenu*.	ಪಟ್ಟಿತು *paṭṭitu*.	ಪಟ್ಟೇನು *paṭṭénu*.
ಬರು *baru*, Come.	ಬಂದು *bandu*.	ಬಂದೆನು *bandenu*.	ಬಂತು *bantu*.	ಬಂದೇನು *bandénu*.
ಬಲಿ *bali*, Become stout.	ಬಲಿತು *balitu*.	ಬಲಿತೆನು *balitenu*.	ಬಲಿಯಿತು *baliyitu*.	ಬಲಿತೇನು *baliténu*.
ಬಸಿ *basi*, Strain.	ಬಸಿದು *basidu*.	ಬಸಿದೆನು *basidenu*.	ಬಸಿಯಿತು *basiyitu*.	ಬಸಿದೇನು *basidénu*.
	ಬಸಿತು *basitu*.	ಬಸಿತೆನು *basitenu*.		ಬಸಿತೇನು *basiténu*.
ಬಾ *bá*, Swell.	ಬಾತು *bátu*.	ಬಾತೆನು *bátenu*.	ಬಾಯಿತು *báyitu*.	ಬಾತೇನು *báténu*.
ಬಿಗು *bigu*, Swell.	ಬಿಕ್ಕು *bikku*.	ಬಿಕ್ಕೆನು *bikkenu*.	ಬಿಕ್ಕಿತು *bikkitu*.	ಬಿಕ್ಕೇನು *bikkénu*.
ಬಿಡು *biḍu*, Put forth.	ಬಿಟ್ಟು *biṭṭu*.	ಬಿಟ್ಟೆನು *biṭṭenu*.	ಬಿಟ್ಟಿತು *biṭṭitu*.	ಬಿಟ್ಟೇನು *biṭṭénu*.

	Past Gerund.	Past Tense. 1st per. sing.	Past Tense. 3rd per. sing. neut.	Con. Future. 1st per. sing.
ಬಿರಿ *biri*, Split.	ಬಿರಿದು *biridu*.	ಬಿರಿದೆನು *biridenu*.	ಬಿರಿಯಿತು *biriyitu*.	ಬಿರಿದೇನು *biridénu*.
	ಬಿರಿತು *biritu*.	ಬಿರಿತೆನು *biritenu*.		ಬಿರಿತೇನು *biriténu*.
ಬಿಸಾಡು *bisáḍu*, Throw away.	ಬಿಸಾಟು *bisáṭu*.	ಬಿಸಾಟೆನು *bisáṭenu*.	ಬಿಸಾಟಿತು *bisáṭitu*.	ಬಿಸಾಟೇನು *bisáṭénu*.
ಬಿಸುಡು *bisuḍu*, Throw away.	ಬಿಸುಡಿ *bisuḍi*.	ಬಿಸುಡಿದೆನು *bisuḍidenu*.	ಬಿಸುಡಿತು *bisuḍitu*.	ಬಿಸುಡಿಯೇನು *bisuḍiyénu*.
	ಬಿಸುಟು *bisuṭu*.	ಬಿಸುಟೆನು *bisuṭenu*.	ಬಿಸುಟಿತು *bisuṭitu*.	ಬಿಸುಟೇನು *bisuṭénu*.
ಬೀ *bí*, (2nd per. sing. Imp. ಬೀಯಿ *bíyi*,) Be past bearing.	ಬೀತು *bítu*.	ಬೀತೆನು *bítenu*.	ಬೀಯಿತು *bíyitu*.	ಬೀತೇನು *biténu*.
ಬೀಳು *bíḷu*, Fall.	ಬಿದ್ದು *biddu*.	ಬಿದ್ದೆನು *biddenu*.	ಬಿತ್ತು *bittu*.	ಬಿದ್ದೇನು *biddénu*.
ಬೆವರು *bevaru*, Perspire.	ಬೆವರ್ತು *bevartu*.	ಬೆವರ್ತೆನು *bevartenu*.	ಬೆವರ್ತಿತು *bevartitu*.	ಬೆವರ್ತೇನು *bevarténu*.
ಬೆಸೆ *bese*, Solder.	ಬೆಸೆದು *besedu*.	ಬೆಸೆದೆನು *besedenu*.	ಬೆಸೆಯಿತು *beseyitu*.	ಬೆಸೆದೇನು *besedénu*.
	ಬೆಸೆತು *besetu*.	ಬೆಸೆತೆನು *besetenu*.		ಬೆಸೆತೇನು *beseténu*.
ಬೇ *bé*, (2nd per. sing. Imp. ಬೇಯಿ *béyi*,) Boil.	ಬೆಂದು *bendu*.	ಬೆಂದೆನು *bendenu*.	ಬೆಂದಿತು *benditu*.	ಬೆಂದೇನು *bendénu*.
ಬೇಸರು *bésaru*, Be tired.	ಬೇಸತ್ತು *bésattu*.	ಬೇಸತ್ತೆನು *bésattenu*.	ಬೇಸತ್ತಿತು *bésattitu*.	ಬೇಸತ್ತೇನು *bésatténu*.
ಮಡು *maḍu*, Strengthen.	ಮಟ್ಟು *maṭṭu*.	ಮಟ್ಟೆನು *maṭṭenu*.	ಮಟ್ಟಿತು *maṭṭitu*.	ಮಟ್ಟೇನು *maṭṭénu*.
ಮಡಲು *maḍalu*, Spread, as a creeper.	ಮಡಲ್ತು *maḍaltu*.	ಮಡಲ್ತೆನು *maḍaltenu*.	ಮಡಲ್ತಿತು *maḍaltitu*.	ಮಡಲ್ತೇನು *maḍalténu*.
ಮರೆ *mare*, Forget.	ಮರೆತು *maretu*.	ಮರೆತೆನು *maretenu*.	ಮರೆಯಿತು *mareyitu*.	ಮರೆತೇನು *mareténu*.
ಮಲೆ *male*, Resist.	ಮಲೆತು *maletu*.	ಮಲೆತೆನು *maletenu*.	ಮಲೆಯಿತು *maleyitu*.	ಮಲೆತೇನು *maleténu*.
ಮಸೆ *mase*, Whet.	ಮಸೆದು *masedu*.	ಮಸೆದೆನು *masedenu*.	ಮಸೆಯಿತು *maseyitu*.	ಮಸೆದೇನು *masedénu*.
	ಮಸೆತು *masetu*.	ಮಸೆತೆನು *masetenu*.		ಮಸೆತೇನು *maseténu*.

		Past Tense.		Con. Future.
	Past Gerund.	1st per. sing.	3rd per. sing. neut.	1st per. sing.
ಮಾ *má*, Heal.	ಮಾದು *mádu*.	ಮಾದೆನು *mádenu*.	ಮಾಯಿತು *máyitu*.	ಮಾದೇನು *mádénu*.
ಮಿಗು *migu*, Exceed.	ಮಿಕ್ಕು *mikku*.	ಮಿಕ್ಕೆನು *mikkenu*.	ಮಿಕ್ಕಿತು *mikkitu*.	ಮಿಕ್ಕೇನು *mikkénu*.
ಮಿದಿ *midi*, Kill.	ಮಿತ್ತು *mittu*.	ಮಿತ್ತೆನು *mittenu*.	ಮಿತ್ತಿತು *mittitu*.	ಮಿತ್ತೇನು *mitténu*.
ಮಿಳಿರು *miḷiru*, Thrive.	ಮಿಳಿರ್ತು *miḷirtu*.	ಮಿಳಿರ್ತೆನು, *miḷirtenu*.	ಮಿಳಿರ್ತಿತು *miḷirtitu*.	ಮಿಳಿರ್ತೇನು *miḷirténu*.
ಮೀ *mí*, (2nd per. sing. Imp. ಮೀಯಿ *míyi*,) Bathe.	ಮಿಂದು *mindu*.	ಮಿಂದೆನು *mindenu*.	ಮಿಂದಿತು *minditu*.	ಮಿಂದೇನು *mindénu*.
ಮುನಿ *muni*, Be angry.	{ ಮುನಿದು *munidu*.	ಮುನಿದೆನು *munidenu*.	ಮುನಿಯಿತು *muniyitu*.	ಮುನಿದೇನು *munidénu*.
	{ ಮುನಿತು *munitu*.	ಮುನಿತೆನು *munitenu*.		ಮುನಿತೇನು *muniténu*.
ಮೆಲ್ಲು *mellu*, Chew.	ಮೆದ್ದು *meddu*.	ಮೆದ್ದೆನು *meddenu*.	ಮೆದ್ದಿತು *medditu*.	ಮೆದ್ದೇನು *meddénu*.
ಮೇ *mé*, Graze.	ಮೇದು *médu*.	ಮೇದೆನು *médenu*.	ಮೇಯಿತು *méyitu*.	ಮೇದೇನು *médénu*.
ಮೊಳೆ *moḷe*, Sprout.	ಮೊಳೆತು *moḷetu*.	ಮೊಳೆತೆನು *moḷetenu*.	ಮೊಳೆಯಿತು *moḷeyitu*.	ಮೊಳೆತೇನು *moḷeténu*.
ಸಲ್ಲು *sallu*. Be current, pass.	ಸಂದು *sandu*.	ಸಂದೆನು *sandenu*.	ಸಂದಿತು, *sanditu*, ಸಂತು *santu*.	ಸಂದೇನು *sandénu*.
ಸಾ *sá*, Die.	ಸತ್ತು *sattu*.	ಸತ್ತೆನು *sattenu*.	ಸತ್ತಿತು *sattitu*.	ಸತ್ತೇನು *satténu*.
ಸಾಲು, *sálu*, Borrow, be in debt.	ಸಾತು *sátu*.	ಸಾತೆನು *sátenu*.	ಸಾತಿತು *sátitu*.	ಸಾತೇನು *sáténu*.
ಸೀನು *sínu*, Sneeze.	ಸೀತು *sítu*.	ಸೀತೆನು *sítenu*.	ಸೀತಿತು *sititu*.	ಸೀತೇನು *siténu*.
ಸುಡು *suḍu*, Burn.	ಸುಟ್ಟು *suṭṭu*.	ಸುಟ್ಟೆನು *suṭṭenu*.	ಸುಟ್ಟಿತು *suṭṭitu*.	ಸುಟ್ಟೇನು *suṭṭénu*.
ಸೋಲು *sólu*, Be defeated.	ಸೋತು *sótu*.	ಸೋತೆನು *sótenu*.	ಸೋತಿತು *sótitu*.	ಸೋತೇನು *sóténu*.
ಹದಿ *hadi*, Pave.	ಹದ್ದು *haddu*.	ಹದ್ದೆನು *haddenu*.	ಹದ್ದಿತು *hadditu*.	ಹದ್ದೇನು *haddénu*.

	Past Gerund.	Past Tense. 1st per. sing.	Past Tense. 3rd per. sing. neut.	Con. Future, 1st per. sing.
ಹಸಿ *hasi*, Be hungry.	ಹಸಿದು *hasidu*.	ಹಸಿದೆನು *hasidenu*,	ಹಸಿಯಿತು *hasiyitu*.	ಹಸಿದೇನು *hasidénu*.
	ಹಸಿತು *hasitu*.	ಹಸಿತೆನು *hasitenu*.		ಹಸಿತೇನು *hasiténu*.
ಹಿಸಿ *hisi*, Split.	ಹಿಸಿದು *hisidu*.	ಹಿಸಿದೆನು *hisidenu*.	ಹಿಸಿಯಿತು *hisiyitu*.	ಹಿಸಿದೇನು *hisidénu*.
	ಹಿಸಿತು *hisitu*.	ಹಿಸಿತೆನು *hisitenu*.		ಹಿಸಿತೇನು *hisiténu*.
ಹುಸಿ *husi*, Lie.	ಹುಸಿದು *husidu*.	ಹುಸಿದೆನು *husidenu*.	ಹುಸಿಯಿತು *husiyitu*.	ಹುಸಿದೇನು *husidénu*.
	ಹುಸಿತು *husitu*.	ಹುಸಿತೆನು *husitenu*.		ಹುಸಿತೇನು *husiténu*.
ಹೆರು *heru*, Bring forth children.	ಹೆತ್ತು *hettu*.	ಹೆತ್ತೆನು *hettenu*.	ಹೆತ್ತಿತು *hettitu*.	ಹೆತ್ತೇನು *hetténu*.
ಹೇಲು *hélu*, Void excrement.	ಹೇತು *hétu*.	ಹೇತೆನು *hétenu*.	ಹೇತಿತು *hétitu*.	ಹೇತೇನು *héténu*.
ಹೊಗು *hogu*, Enter.	ಹೊಕ್ಕು *hokku*.	ಹೊಕ್ಕೆನು *hokkenu*.	ಹೊಕ್ಕಿತು *hokkitu*.	ಹೊಕ್ಕೇನು *hokkénu*.
ಹೊದಿ *hodi*, Put on clothes, cover.	ಹೊದ್ದು *hoddu*.	ಹೊದ್ದೆನು *hoddenu*.	ಹೊದ್ದಿತು *hodditu*.	ಹೊದ್ದೇನು *hoddénu*.
ಹೊರಡು *horaḍu*, Set out.	ಹೊರಟು *horaṭu*.	ಹೊರಟೆನು *horaṭenu*.	ಹೊರಟಿತು *horaṭitu*.	ಹೊರಟೇನು *horaṭénu*.
ಹೊರು *horu*, Bear a burden.	ಹೊತ್ತು *hottu*.	ಹೊತ್ತೆನು *hottenu*.	ಹೊತ್ತಿತು *hottitu*.	ಹೊತ್ತೇನು *hotténu*.
ಹೊಸೆ *hose*, Twist.	ಹೊಸೆದು *hosedu*.	ಹೊಸೆದೆನು *hosedenu*.	ಹೊಸೆಯಿತು *hoseyitu*.	ಹೊಸೆದೇನು *hosedénu*.
	ಹೊಸೆತು *hosetu*.	ಹೊಸೆತೆನು *hosetenu*.		ಹೊಸೆತೇನು *hoseténu*.
ಹೋಗು *hógu*, Go.	ಹೋಗಿ *hógi*.	ಹೋದೆನು *hódenu*.	ಹೋಯಿತು *hóyitu*.	ಹೋದೇನು *hódénu*.
ಹೋಲು *hólu*, Resemble.	ಹೋತು *hótu*.	ಹೋತೆನು *hótenu*.	ಹೋತಿತು *hótitu*.	ಹೋತೇನು *hóténu*.

117. The following verbs are irregular in the 2nd per. sing. imper. only.

Root.	2nd per. sing. IMPERATIVE.
ಆರಯು *árayu*, Search.	ಆರಯಿ *árayi*.
ಆಯು *áyu*, Select.	ಆಯಿ *áyi*.
ಒಯು *oyu*, Carry.	ಒಯಿ *oyi*.
ಕಾ *ká* Guard.	ಕಾಯಿ *káyi*.
ಕಾಯು *káyu*, Bear fruit.	ಕಾಯಿ *káyi*.
ಕೊಯು *koyu*, } Cut.	ಕೊಯಿ *koyi*.
ಕೊಯ್ಯು *koyyu*, } Cut.	ಕೊಯ್ಯಿ *koyyi*.
ಕೈಗಾಯು *keigáyu*, Protect.	ಕೈಗಾಯಿ *keigáyi*.
ಗೇಯು *géyu*, Make.	ಗೇಯಿ *géyi*.
ತೋ *tó*, Wet.	ತೋಯಿ *tóyi*.
ನೇಯು *néyu*, Weave.	ನೇಯಿ *néyi*.
ಬಯು *bayu*, } Abuse.	ಬಯಿ *bayi*.
ಬಯ್ಯು *bayyu*, } Abuse.	ಬಯ್ಯಿ *bayyi*.
ಮಾ *má*, Heal.	ಮಾಯಿ *máyi*.
ಮೇ *mé*, Feed.	ಮೇಯಿ *méyi*.
ಸುಯ್ಯು *suyyu*, Sigh.	ಸುಯ್ಯಿ *suyyi*.
ಹಾಯು *háyu*, Cross over.	ಹಾಯಿ *háyi*.
ಹೊಯ್ಯು *hoyyu*, Beat.	ಹೊಯ್ಯಿ *hoyyi*.

CONJUGATION OF IRREGULAR VERBS.

118. Root, ಇರು *iru*, Be, exist, &c. (282.)

GERUNDS, or verbal participles.

		The root, and
Present.	ಇರುತ್ತ *irutta*, being.	ಉತ್ತ *utta*.
	ಇರುತ್ತಾ *iruttá*, „	ಉತ್ತಾ *uttá*.
Past.	ಇದ್ದು *iddu*, having been. *	Irregular.
Negative.	ಇರದೆ *irade*, not having been.	ಅದೆ *ade*.

RELATIVE PARTICIPLES.

		The root and
Pres. & Fut.	ಇರುವ *iruva*, who or which is, or will be.	ಉವ *uva*.
Past.	ಇದ್ದ *idda*, who or which was.	* Irregular.
Negative.	ಇರದ *irada*, { who or which is not, was not, or will not be.	ಅದ *ada*.

* Whenever the past gerund is irregular, the past relative participle is always formed from it, by changing the final ಉ *u*, into ಅ *a*. Thus, *iddu*, having been, becomes *idda*, who or which was.

Compound Relative Participles.

Pres. & Future.	ಇರುತ್ತಿರುವ *iruttiruva,*	who or which is, or will be.	Present gerund and present relative participle.
Past.	ಇರುತ್ತಿದ್ದ *iruttidda,*	who or which was existing.	Present gerund and past relative participle.

INFINITIVE MOOD.

		The root, and
ಇರ *ira,*	to be.	ಅ *a.*
ಇರಲು *iralu,*		ಅಲು *alu.*
ಇರಲಿಕ್ಕೆ *iralikke,*		ಅಲಿಕ್ಕೆ *alikke.*

IMPERATIVE MOOD.

(Root and personal affixes.)

Let me, &c. be.

	Singular.	Plural.
1st per.	ಇರಲಿ *irali,* let me be.	ಇರಲಿ *irali,* let us be.
2nd.	ಇರು *iru,* be thou.	ಇರಿ *iri,* be ye.
3rd.	ಇರಲಿ *irali,* let him be.	ಇರಲಿ *irali,* let them be.

NEGATIVE MOOD.

(Root and personal affixes.)

I, &c. am not, was not, or shall not be.

	Singular.	Plural.
1st per.	ಇರೆನು *irenu,* I, &c.	ಇರೆವು *irevu,* we, &c.
2nd.	ಇರೆ *ire,* thou, &c.	ಇರರಿ *irari,* ye, &c.
3rd mas.	ಇರನು *iranu,* he, &c.	ಇರರು *iraru,* they, &c.
3rd fem.	ಇರಳು *iraḷu,* she, &c.	ಇರರು *iraru,* ,,
3rd neut.	ಇರದು *iradu,* it, &c.	ಇರವು *iravu,* ,,

AFFIRMATIVE MOOD.

Present Tense. 1st Form. I am, &c.

(Present Gerund ಇರುತ್ತ *irutta,* and personal affixes.)

1st per.	ಇರುತ್ತೇನೆ *irutténe,* I am.	ಇರುತ್ತೇವೆ *iruttéve,* we are.
2nd.	ಇರುತ್ತೀ *irutti,* thou art.	ಇರುತ್ತೀರಿ *iruttíri,* ye are.

	Singular.	Plural.
3rd m.	ಇರುತ್ತಾನೆ *iruttáne*, he is.	ಇರುತ್ತಾರೆ *iruttáre*, they are.
3rd f.	ಇರುತ್ತಾಳೆ *iruttáḷe*, she is.	ಇರುತ್ತಾರೆ *iruttáre*, ,,
3rd n.	ಇರುತ್ತದೆ *iruttade*, it is.	ಇರುತ್ತವೆ *iruttave*, ,,

Present Tense. 2nd Form. I am, &c.

(Irregular ಇದ್ಧ *iddha*, and the same personal affixes as the preceding form.)

1st per.	ಇದ್ಧೇನೆ *iddhéne*, I am.	ಇದ್ಧೇವೆ *iddhéve*, we are.
2nd.	ಇದ್ಧೀ *iddhí*, thou art.	ಇದ್ಧೀರಿ *iddhíri*, ye are.
3rd m.	ಇದ್ಧಾನೆ *iddháne*, he is.	ಇದ್ಧಾರೆ *iddháre*, they are.
3rd f.	ಇದ್ಧಾಳೆ *iddháḷe*, she is.	ಇದ್ಧಾರೆ *iddháre*, ,,
3rd n.	ಇದೆ *ide*, it is. } Irregular. ಅದೆ *ade*, ,,	ಇವೆ *ive*, ,, } Irregular. ಅವೆ *ave*, ,,

Past Tense. I was, &c.

(Past relative participle and personal affixes.)

1st Per.	ಇದ್ದೆನು *iddenu*, I was.	ಇದ್ದೆವು *iddevu*, we were.
2nd.	ಇದ್ದಿ *iddi*, thou wast. ಇದ್ದೆ *idde*, ,,	ಇದ್ದಿರಿ *iddiri*, ye were.
3rd m.	ಇದ್ದನು *iddanu*, he was.	ಇದ್ದರು *iddaru*, they were.
3rd f.	ಇದ್ದಳು *iddaḷu*, she was.	ಇದ್ದರು *iddaru*, ,,
3rd n.	ಇತ್ತು *ittu*, it was.	ಇದ್ದವು *iddavu*, ,,

1st Future Tense. I shall or will be, &c.

(Future relative participle ಇರುವ *iruva*, and personal affixes.)

	Singular.	Plural.
1st per.	ಇರುವೆನು *iruvenu*, I, &c.	ಇರುವೆವು *iruvevu*, we, &c.
2nd.	ಇರುವಿ *iruvi*, thou, &c. ಇರುವೆ *iruve*, ,,	ಇರುವಿರಿ *iruviri*, ye, &c.
3rd m.	ಇರುವನು *iruvanu*, he, &c.	ಇರುವರು *iruvaru*, they, &c.
3rd f.	ಇರುವಳು *iruvaḷu*, she, &c.	ಇರುವರು *iruvaru*, ,,
3rd n.	ಇರುವದು *iruvadu*, it, &c.	ಇರುವವು *iruvavu*, ,,

2nd or CONTINGENT FUTURE TENSE. I shall perhaps, or, I may be.

(Past gerund ಇದ್ದು *iddu,* and personal affixes.)

1st per.	ಇದ್ದೇನು *iddénu*, I, &c.	ಇದ್ದೇವು *iddévu*, we, &c.
2nd.	ಇದ್ದೀಯೇ *iddíyé*, thou, &c.	ಇದ್ದೀರಿ *iddíri*, ye, &c.
3rd m.	ಇದ್ದಾನು *iddánu*, he, &c.	ಇದ್ದಾರು *iddáru*, they, &c.
3rd f.	ಇದ್ದಾಳು *iddáḷu*, she, &c.	ಇದ್ದಾರು *iddáru*, ,,
3rd n.	ಇದ್ದೀತು *idditu*, it, &c.	ಇದ್ದಾವು *iddávu*, ,,

POTENTIAL MOOD.

(The infinitive mood ಇರ *ira,* to be, and auxiliary verbs.)

ಇರ ಬಹುದು *ira-bahudu,* I, &c. may be.
ಇರ ಬಾರದು *ira-báradu,* I, &c. may not be.
(&c. &c. as in verbs of the 1st conjugation.)

SUBJUNCTIVE MOOD.

AORIST TENSE. Impersonal.

(Past rel. part. ಇದ್ದ *idda,* and the affixes ರೆ *re,* ರೂ *rú,* and ಆಗ್ಯೂ *ágyú.*)

ಇದ್ದರೆ *iddare,* If I, &c. am, were, shall or should be.
ಇದ್ದರೂ *iddarú,* } Although I, &c. am, were, shall or should be.
ಇದ್ದಾಗ್ಯೂ *iddágyú,* }

PRESENT AND FUTURE TENSE.

(Pres. and fut. rel. part. ಇರುವ *iruva,* and ಹಾಗೆ *háge,* that, so that.)
ಇರುವ ಹಾಗೆ *iruva-háge,* that I, &c. may or might be.

NEGATIVE.

(Negative relative participle ಇರದ *irada,* and ಹಾಗೆ *háge,* that, so that.)
ಇರದ ಹಾಗೆ *irada-háge,* that I, &c. may not, or might not be.

---

119. The Irregular verb ಆಗು *águ,* Become. * (269—281.)

GERUNDS, OR VERBAL PARTICIPLES.

		The root and
Present.	ಆಗುತ್ತ *águtta,* becoming.	ಉತ್ತ *utta.*
	or ಆಗುತ್ತಾ *águttá,* ,,	ಉತ್ತಾ *uttá.*
Past.	ಆಗಿ *ági,* having become.	ಇ *i.*
Negative.	ಆಗದೆ *ágade,* not having become.	ಅದೆ *ade.*

* ಹೋಗು *hógu,* go, is conjugated exactly like ಆಗು *águ.* Put ಹೋ *hó,* in the place of ಆ *á,* and this example will do for both verbs. (302.)

Relative Participles.

		The root and
Pres. & Future.	ಆಗುವ *águva*, who or which becomes, or will become.	ಉವ *uva*.
Past.	ಆದ *ada*, who or which became.	Irregular.
Negative.	ಆಗದ *ágada*, who or which becomes not, became not, or will not become.	ಅದ *ada*.

Compound Relative Participles.

		Present gerund and
Pres. & Future.	ಆಗುತ್ತಿರುವ *águttiruva*, who or which is becoming, or will be becoming.	ಇರುವ *iruva*.
Past.	ಆಗುತ್ತಿದ್ದ *águttidda*, who or which was becoming.	ಇದ್ದ *idda*.
		Past Gerund and
Perf. & fut. per.	ಆಗಿರುವ *ágiruva*, who or which has become, or will have become.	ಇರುವ *iruva*.
Pluperfect.	ಆಗಿದ್ದ *ágidda*, who or which had become.	ಇದ್ದ *idda*.

INFINITIVE MOOD.

		The Root and
ಆಗ *ága*,	to become.	ಅ *a*.
ಆಗಲು *ágalu*,		ಅಲು *alu*.
ಆಗಲಿಕ್ಕೆ *ágalikke*,		ಅಲಿಕ್ಕೆ *alikke*.

IMPERATIVE MOOD. Let me, &c. become.

(Root and personal affixes.)

Let me, &c. become.

	Singular.	Plural.
1st Per.	ಆಗಲಿ *ágali*.	ಆಗಲಿ *ágali*.
2nd.	ಆಗು *águ*.	ಆಗಿರಿ *ágiri*.
3rd m. f. n.	ಆಗಲಿ *ágali*.	ಆಗಲಿ *ágali*.

NEGATIVE MOOD.

(Root and personal affixes.)

I, &c. do not, did not, or shall not become.

	Singular.	Plural.
1st Per.	ಆಗೆನು *ágenu*.	ಆಗೆವು *ágevu*.
2nd.	ಆಗೆ *áge*.	ಆಗರಿ *ágari*.
3rd m.	ಆಗನು *áganu*.	ಆಗರು *ágaru*.
3rd f.	ಆಗಳು *ágaḷu*.	ಆಗರು *ágaru*.
3rd n.	ಆಗದು *ágadu*.	ಆಗವು *ágavu*.

AFFIRMATIVE MOOD.

PRESENT TENSE. I, &c. become.

(Present gerund ಆಗುತ್ತ *águtta*, and personal affixes.)

1st Per.	ಆಗುತ್ತೇನೆ *águtténe.*	ಆಗುತ್ತೇವೆ *águttéve.*
2nd.	ಆಗುತ್ತೀ *águttí.* ಆಗುತ್ತೀಯೆ *águttíye.*	ಆಗುತ್ತೀರಿ *águttíri.*
3rd m.	ಆಗುತ್ತಾನೆ *águttáne.*	ಆಗುತ್ತಾರೆ *águttáre.*
3rd f.	ಆಗುತ್ತಾಳೆ *águttáḷe.*	ಆಗುತ್ತಾರೆ *águttáre.*
3rd. n.	ಆಗುತ್ತದೆ *águttade.*	ಆಗುತ್ತವೆ *águttave.*

PAST TENSE. I, &c. became.

(Irregular past relative participle ಆದ *áda*, and personal affixes.)

1st Per.	ಆದೆನು *ádenu.*	ಆದೆವು *ádevu.*
2nd.	ಆದಿ *ádi.* ಆದೆ *áde.*	ಆದಿರಿ *ádiri.*
3rd m.	ಆದನು *ádanu.*	ಆದರು *ádaru.*
3rd f.	ಆದಳು *ádaḷu.*	ಆದರು *ádaru.*
3rd n.	ಆಯಿತು *áyitu.*	ಆದವು *ádavu.*

1st FUTURE TENSE. I, &c. shall or will become.

(Future relative participle ಆಗುವ *águva*, and personal affixes.)

1st Per.	ಆಗುವೆನು *águvenu.*	ಆಗುವೆವು *águvevu.*
2nd.	ಆಗುವಿ *águvi.* ಆಗುವೆ *águve.*	ಆಗುವಿರಿ *águviri.*
3rd m.	ಆಗುವನು *águvanu.*	ಆಗುವರು *águvaru.*
3rd f.	ಆಗುವಳು *águvaḷu.*	ಆಗುವರು *águvaru.*
3rd n.	ಆಗುವದು *águvadu.*	ಆಗುವವು *águvavu.*

2nd or CONTINGENT FUTURE. I, &c. shall perhaps, or may become.

(ಆದು *ádu*, instead of ಆಗಿ *ágí*, the regular past gerund, and personal affixes.).

	SINGULAR.	PLURAL.
1st Per.	ಆದೇನು *ádénu.*	ಆದೇವು *ádévu.*
2nd.	ಆದೀಯೆ *ádíye.*	ಆದೀರಿ *ádíri.*
3rd m.	ಆದಾನು *ádánu.*	ಆದಾರು *ádáru.*
3rd f.	ಆದಾಳು *ádáḷu.*	ಆದಾರು *ádáru.*
3rd n.	ಆದೀತು *ádítu.*	ಆದಾವು *ádávu.*

N. B. The compound Tenses, and the Potential and Subjunctive moods are formed according to rule, like verbs of the First conjugation.

120. The verbs ಅನ್ನು *annu*, or ಎನ್ನು *yennu*, Say; and ತಿನ್ನು *tinnu*, Eat, are conjugated as follows. The Tenses not given below are formed according to rule.

ROOT, ಅನ್ನು *annu*, Say. (284—290.)

GERUNDS.

Past. ಅಂದು *andu*, having said.

RELATIVE PARTICIPLES.

Pres. & Fut. ಅನ್ನುವ *annuva*, (regular,) or ಅಂಬ *amba*, (irregular,) who or which says, or will say.

Past. ಅಂದ *anda*, who or which said.

AFFIRMATIVE MOOD.

PRESENT TENSE. This tense is regularly formed; but, in addition, the word ಅಂತೆ *ante*, "They say," "It is said," &c. is of very common use.

PAST TENSE. I said, &c.

(Irregular past rel. part. ಅಂದು *andu*, and the regular personal affixes.)

	SINGULAR.	PLURAL.
1st per.	ಅಂದೆನು *andenu*, I said.	ಅಂದೆವು *andevu*, we said.
2nd.	ಅಂದಿ *andi*, thou saidst.	ಅಂದಿರಿ *andiri*, ye said.
	ಅಂದೆ *ande*, „	
3rd m.	ಅಂದನು *andanu*, he said.	ಅಂದರು *andaru*, they said.
3rd f.	ಅಂದಳು *andaḷu*, she said.	ಅಂದರು *andaru*, „
3rd n.	ಅಂದಿತು *anditu*, it said.	ಅಂದವು *andavu*, „

1st FUTURE TENSE. I shall or will say.

This tense may be regularly formed by adding the usual personal affixes to the *regular* future relative participle, ಅನ್ನುವ *annuva*. Thus,

	SINGULAR.	PLURAL.
1st per.	ಅನ್ನುವೆನು *annuvenu*, I shall say.	ಅನ್ನುವೆವು *annuvevu*, we, &c.
2nd.	ಅನ್ನುವಿ *annuvi*, thou, &c.	ಅನ್ನುವಿರಿ *annuviri*, ye, &c.
	&c. &c.	&c. &c.

Or by adding the same affixes to the *irregular* fut. part. ಅಂಬ *amba*, Thus:—

H

	Singular.	Plural.
1st per.	ಅಂಬೆನು *ambenu.*	ಅಂಬೆವು *ambevu.*
2nd.	ಅಂಬಿ *ambi.*	ಅಂಬಿರಿ *ambiri.*
3rd m.	ಅಂಬನು *ambanu.*	ಅಂಬರು *ambaru.*
3rd f.	ಅಂಬಳು *ambaḷu.*	ಅಂಬರು *ambaru.*
3rd n.	ಅಂಬದು *ambadu.*	ಅಂಬವು *ambavu.*

2nd or Contingent Future. I shall perhaps say.

(Irregular past gerund ಅಂದು *andu,* and the usual personal affixes.)

1st per.	ಅಂದೇನು *andénu.*	ಅಂದೇವು *andévu.*
2nd.	ಅಂದೀಯೆ.	ಅಂದೀರಿ *andíri.*
3rd m.	ಅಂದಾನು *andánu.*	ಅಂದಾರು *andáru.*
3rd f.	ಅಂದಾಳು *andáḷu.*	ಅಂದಾರು *andáru.*
3rd n.	ಅಂದೀತು *andítu.*	ಅಂದಾವು *andávu.*

121. The verbs ಬರು *baru,* Come, and ತರು *taru,* Bring, are conjugated as follows. The tenses not given below are formed according to rule.

Root, ಬರು *baru,* Come. (297.)

Gerunds.

Past. ಬಂದು *bandu,* having come.
Negative. ಬಾರದೆ *bárade,* not having come.

Relative Participles.

Past. ಬಂದ *banda,* who or which came.
Negative. ಬಾರದ *bárada,* who or which comes not, came not, or will not come.

IMPERATIVE MOOD.

	Singular.	Plural.
2nd per.	ಬಾ *bá,* come thou.	ಬನ್ನಿ *banni,* ಬನ್ನಿರಿ *banniri,* come ye.

NEGATIVE MOOD.

I come not, came not, or will not come.

1st per.	ಬಾರೆನು *bárenu,* I, &c.	ಬಾರೆವು *bárevu,* we, &c.
2nd.	ಬಾರೆ *báre,* thou, &c.	ಬಾರಿರಿ *báriri,* ye, &c.

	SINGULAR.	PLURAL.
3rd. m.	ಬಾರನು *báranu*, he, &c.	ಬಾರರು *báraru*, they, &c.
3rd f.	ಬಾರಳು *báraḷu*, she, &c.	ಬಾರರು *báraru*, „
3rd n.	ಬಾರದು *báradu*, it, &c.	ಬಾರವು *báravu*, „

AFFIRMATIVE MOOD.

PAST TENSE. I, &c. came.

(Irregular past. rel. part. ಬಂದ *bandu*, and personal affixes.)

1st per.	ಬಂದೆನು *bandenu*, I came.	ಬಂದೆವು *bandevu*, we came.
2nd.	ಬಂದೆ *bande*, thou camest.	ಬಂದಿರಿ *bandiri*, ye came.
3rd m.	ಬಂದನು *bandanu*, he came.	ಬಂದರು *bandaru*, they came.
3rd f.	ಬಂದಳು *bandaḷu*, she came.	ಬಂದರು *bandaru*, „
3rd n.	ಬಂತು *bantu*, it came.	ಬಂದವು *bandavu*, „

2nd or CONTINGENT FUTURE. I shall perhaps come.

(Irregular past gerund ಬಂದು *bandu*, and personal affixes.)

1st per.	ಬಂದೇನು *bandénu*, I, &c.	ಬಂದೇವು *bandévu*, we, &c.
2nd.	ಬಂದೀಯೆ *bandíye*, thou, &c.	ಬಂದೀರಿ *bandíri*, ye, &c.
3rd m.	ಬಂದಾನು *bandánu*, he, &c.	ಬಂದಾರು *bandáru*, they, &c.
3rd f.	ಬಂದಾಳು *bandáḷu*, she, &c.	ಬಂದಾರು *bandáru*, „
3rd n.	ಬಂದೀತು *bandítu*, it, &c.	ಬಂದಾವು *bandávu*, „

DEFECTIVE VERBS.

122. A few verbs are defective as well as irregular. They are conjugated as follows :—

123. ಆಪ *ápa*, is used as an auxiliary verb, to denote ability.

GERUNDS.

Negative. ಆರದೆ *árade*, not having been able.

RELATIVE PARTICIPLES.

Pres. & Fut. ಆಪುವ *ápuva*, who or which can, or is able.

Negative. ಆರದ *árada*, who or which cannot, or is not able.

AFFIRMATIVE MOOD.

Present, Past, and Future Tense.

I, &c. am, was, or shall be able.

	Singular.	Plural.
1st per.	ಆಪೆನು *ápenu*, I, &c.	ಆಪೆವು *ápevu*, we, &c.
2nd.	ಆಪಿ *ápi*, ಆಪೆ *ápe*, thou, &c.	ಆಪಿರಿ *ápiri*, ye, &c.
3rd m.	ಆಪನು *ápanu*, he, &c.	ಆಪರು *áparu*, they, &c.
3rd f.	ಆಪಳು *ápaḷu*, she, &c.	ಆಪರು *áparu*, ,,
3rd n.	ಆಪದು *ápadu*, it, &c.	ಆಪವು *ápavu*, ,,

NEGATIVE MOOD.

I, &c. am not, was not, or shall not be able.

1st per.	ಆರೆನು *árenu*, I, &c.	ಆರೆವು *árevu*, we, &c.
2nd.	ಆರಿ *ári*, ಆರೆ *áre*, thou, &c.	ಆರಿರಿ *áriri*, ye, &c.
3rd m.	ಆರನು *áranu*, he, &c.	ಆರರು *áraru*, they, &c.
3rd f.	ಆರಳು *áraḷu*, she, &c.	ಆರರು *áraru*, ,,
3rd n.	ಆರದು *áradu*, it, &c.	ಆರವು *áravu*, ,,

124. ಬಲ್ಲ *balla*, is used as an auxiliary verb to denote ability.

Relative Participle.

Present & Future. } ಬಲ್ಲ *balla*, who or which knows, can, or is able.

AFFIRMATIVE MOOD.

Present, Past, and Future Tense.

I, &c. know, can, am able, was able, or shall be able.

	Singular.	Plural.
1st per.	ಬಲ್ಲೆನು *ballenu*, I, &c.	ಬಲ್ಲೆವು *ballevu*, we, &c.
2nd.	ಬಲ್ಲಿ *balli*, ಬಲ್ಲೆ *balle*, thou, &c.	ಬಲ್ಲಿರಿ *balliri*, ye, &c.
3rd m.	ಬಲ್ಲನು *ballanu*, he, &c.	ಬಲ್ಲರು *ballaru*, they, &c.
3rd f.	ಬಲ್ಲಳು *ballaḷu*, she, &c.	ಬಲ್ಲರು *ballaru*, ,,
3rd n.	ಬಲ್ಲದು *balladu*, it, &c.	ಬಲ್ಲವು *ballavu*, ,,

125. This verb has no negative mood. The deficiency is supplied by the negative of ಅರಿ *ari*, know, (an irregular, but not defective verb,) which is used as an auxiliary in the potential mood of regular verbs.

I, &c. know not, cannot, am not able, was not able, and shall not be able.

	SINGULAR.	PLURAL.
1st per.	ಅರಿಯೆನು *ariyenu*, I, &c.	ಅರಿಯೆವು *ariyevu*, we, &c.
2nd.	ಅರಿಯೆ *ariye*, thou, &c.	ಅರಿಯರಿ *ariyari*, ye, &c.
3rd m.	ಅರಿಯನು *ariyanu*, he, &c.	ಅರಿಯರು *ariyaru*, they, &c.
3rd f.	ಅರಿಯಳು *ariyaḷu*, she, &c.	ಅರಿಯರು *ariyaru*, ,,
3rd n.	ಅರಿಯದು *ariyadu*, it, &c.	ಅರಿಯವು *ariyavu*, ,,

126. ಒಲ್ಲು *ollu*, denotes want of consent. It takes the personal affixes only.

AFFIRMATIVE MOOD, Present, Past, and Future Tense.

I, &c. consent not, I will not, &c.

1st per.	ಒಲ್ಲೆನು *ollenu*, I, &c.	ಒಲ್ಲೆವು *ollevu*, we, &c.
2nd.	ಒಲ್ಲೆ *olle*, thou, &c.	ಒಲ್ಲಿರಿ *olliri*, ye, &c.
3rd m.	ಒಲ್ಲನು *ollanu*, he, &c.	ಒಲ್ಲರು *ollaru*, they, &c.
3rd f.	ಒಲ್ಲಳು *ollaḷu*, she, &c.	ಒಲ್ಲರು *ollaru*, ,,
3rd n.	ಒಲ್ಲದು *olladu*, it, &c.	ಒಲ್ಲವು *ollavu*, ,,

127. The following verbs are *impersonal*, as well as defective in Tenses, &c.

ಉಂಟು *uṇṭu*, there is, it exists, they exist, &c.

GERUNDS.

Negative. ಇಲ್ಲದೆ *illade*, not existing, or not having existed.

RELATIVE PARTICIPLES.

Pres. & Fut. ಉಳ್ಳ *uḷḷa*, who or which does, or will, exist.
Negative. ಇಲ್ಲದ *illada*, who or which does not, did not, or will not, exist.

AFFIRMATIVE MOOD.

Present, Past, and Future Tense.

ಉಂಟು *uṇṭu*, It exists, or, they exist.

NEGATIVE MOOD.

ಇಲ್ಲ *illa*, It does not exist, or, they do not exist, &c.

ಇಲ್ಲ *illa*, is added to the Infinitive in ಲು *lu*, to denote negation in the past tense; as, ಅವನು ಕೇಳಲಿಲ್ಲ *avanu kéḷalilla*, he did not hear.

128. ಅಹುದು *ahudu*, or ಹೌದು *houdu*, from the ancient Canarese ಅಹು *ahu*, be, exist, &c. is used in the sense of yes, it is, or, they are, of that nature and quality.

Gerunds.

Negative. ಅಲ್ಲದೆ *allade*, not being of that nature, &c.

Relative Participles.

Negative. ಅಲ್ಲದ *allada*, who or which does not, did not, or will not be of that nature, &c.

AFFIRMATIVE MOOD.

Present, Past, and Future Tenses.

ಅಹುದು *ahudu*, or ಹೌದು *houdu*, he or it, &c. is, or will be, of that nature or quality.

NEGATIVE MOOD.

ಅಲ್ಲ *alla*, he or it, &c. is not, was not, or will not be of that nature or quality.

129. The following verbs are used impersonally in forming the potential mood, &c.

ಕೂಡುವದು *kúḍuwadu*,	May.	Affirmative Mood, Future Tense, 3rd per. sing. neut. of ಕೂಡು *kúḍu*, join.
ಕೂಡದು *kúḍadu*,	May not.	Negative Mood, 3rd per. sing. neut. of ಕೂಡು *kúḍu*, join, be united, &c.
ತಕ್ಕದ್ದು *takkaddu*,	Ought.	From ತಕ್ಕ *takka*, suitable, fit, proper.
ಬಹುದು *bahudu*,	May.	Ancient form of Affirmative Mood, Future Tense, 3rd per. sing. neut. of the obsolete word ಬಹು *bahu*, come.
ಬಾರದು *báradu*,	May not.	Negative Mood, 3rd per. sing. neut. of ಬರು *baru*, come.
ಬೇಕು *béku*,	Must.	
ಬೇಡ *béḍa*,	Must not.	
ಸಾಕು *sáku*,	Enough.	

ADVERBS.

130. Adverbs are generally formed by the addition ಆಗಿ *ági*, to nouns and adjectives; as, ಅಂದ *anda*, beauty, ಅಂದವಾಗಿ *andawági*, beautifully; ಸಂತೋಷ *santóṣha*, gladness, ಸಂತೋಷವಾಗಿ *santóṣhawági*. gladly. ಗುಪ್ತ *gupta*, secret, ಗುಪ್ತವಾಗಿ *guptawági*, secretly; ನೀಟು *níṭu*, straight, ನೀಟಾಗಿ *níṭági*, straightly.

131. Some adverbs are declined like nouns in the singular number; as,

ಆಗ *ága*, then, that time.

Nom. ಆಗ *ága*, ಆಗಲು *ágalu*, then.

Ins. ಆಗಿನಿಂದ *ágininda*, ಆಗಲಿಂದ *ágalinda*, thence.

Dat. ಆಗ್ಯೆ *ágye*, at that time.

Gen. ಆಗಿನ *ágina*, ಆಗಲಿನ *ágalina*, of that time.

Lo. ಆಗಿನಲ್ಲಿ *áginalli*, ಆಗಲಲ್ಲಿ *ágalalli*, in or at that time.

In like manner are declined ಈಗ *íga*, ಈಗಲು *ígalu*, now; ಯಾವಾಗ *yáwága*, ಯಾವಾಗಲು *yáwágalu*, when; ಸುತ್ತ *sutta*, ಸುತ್ತಲು *suttalu*, around; ಅತ್ತ *atta*, ಅತ್ತಲು *attalu*, that side; ಇತ್ತ *itta*, ಇತ್ತಲು *ittalu*, this side; ಎತ್ತ *yetta*, ಎತ್ತಲು *yettalu*, which side.

132. ನಿನ್ನೆ *ninne*, yesterday.

Nom. ನಿನ್ನೆ *ninne*, yesterday.

Ac. ನಿನ್ನೆಯನ್ನು *ninneyannu*, yesterday.

Ins. ನಿನ್ನೆಯಿಂದ *ninneyinda*, from yesterday.

Dat. ನಿನ್ನೆಗೆ *ninnege*, yesterday.

Gen. ನಿನ್ನೆಯ *ninneya*, ನಿನ್ನಿನ *ninnina*, of yesterday.

Lo. ನಿನ್ನೆಯಲ್ಲಿ *ninneyalli*, yesterday.

133. In like manner are declined ಮೊನ್ನೆ *monne*, the day before yesterday, ನಾಳೆ *náḷe*, to-morrow, ಹೊತಾರೆ *hotáre*, the morning time, ಮುಂಜಾನೆ *munjáne*, the first morning watch, ಬೆಳಿಗ್ಗೆ *beḷigge*, the morning, ಬಯಿಗೆ *baige*, the evening, &c.

134. ನಾಳಿದ್ದು *náḷiddu*, the day after to-morrow.

Nom. ನಾಳಿದ್ದು *náḷiddu*, the day, &c.

Ac. ನಾಳಿದ್ದನ್ನು *náḷiddannu*, the, &c.

Ins. ನಾಳಿದ್ದರಿಂದ *náḷiddarinda*, from the, &c.

Dat. ನಾಳಿದ್ದಕ್ಕೆ *náḷiddakke*, to or for the, &c.

Ab. ನಾಳಿದ್ದರಿಡೆಸೆಯಿಂದ *náḷiddara-deseyinda*, from the, &c.

Gen. ನಾಳಿದ್ದರ *náḷiddara*, of the, &c.

Lo. ನಾಳಿದ್ದರಲ್ಲಿ *náḷiddaralli*, in the, &c.

135. ಬಳಿ *baḷi*, near, nearness.

No. ಬಳಿ *baḷi*, near.
Ac. ಬಳಿಯನ್ನು *baḷiyannu*, nearness.
Ins. ಬಳಿಯಿಂದ *baḷiyinda*, from, away from.
Dat. ಬಳಿಗೆ *baḷige*, to, towards.
Gen. ಬಳಿಯ *baḷiya*, near.
Loc. ಬಳಿಯಲ್ಲಿ *baḷiyalli*, near, at, with.

136. ಅಂದು *andu*, that day, then.

No. ಅಂದು *andu*, that day.
Ac. ಅಂದು *andu*, „
Ins. ಅಂದಿನಿಂದ *andininda*, from that day, thenceforward.
Dat. ಅಂದಿಗೆ *andige*, at that day.
Ab. ಅಂದಿನದೆಸೆಯಿಂದ *andina-deseyinda*, from that day.
Gen. ಅಂದಿನ *andina*, of that day.
Loc. ಅಂದಿನಲ್ಲಿ *andinalli*, in or on that day.

In like manner are declined ಇಂದು *indu*, to day, ಎಂದು *yendu*, what day?

137. ಅಲ್ಲಿ *alli*, there, in that place.

No. ಅಲ್ಲಿ *alli*, there.
Ins. ಅಲ್ಲಿಂದ *allinda*, thence.
Dat. ಅಲ್ಲಿಗೆ *allige*, to there.
Ge. ಅಲ್ಲಿಯ *alliya*, of that place.
Lo. ಅಲ್ಲಿ *alli*, in that place.

In like manner are declined ಇಲ್ಲಿ *illi*, here, this place, and ಎಲ್ಲಿ *yelli*, where, what place?

138. ಹೊರಗು *horagu*, outside.

No. ಹೊರಗು *horagu*, outside.
Ins. ಹೊರಗಿನಿಂದ *horagininda*, from outside.
Dat. ಹೊರಕ್ಕೆ *horakke*, ಹೊರಗೆ *horage*, } to the outside.
Ge. ಹೊರಗಿನ *horagina*, outer.
Lo. ಹೊರಗಿನಲ್ಲಿ *horaginalli*, on the outside.

In like manner are declined ನಡುವು *naḍuvu*, the middle; ಒಳಗು *woḷagu*, the inside; ಕೆಳಗು *keḷagu*, the underside; ಮೇಗು *mégu*, the upper side; ಮುಂದು *mundu*, the front, and ಹಿಂದು *hindu*, the back.

139. The following are some of the indeclinable adverbs.

ಅಂತ *anta,* ಅಂತಲು *antalu,* than, (as an affix.)

ಅಂತ *anta,* ಅಂತಾ *antá,* ಅಂಥ *antha,* ಅಂಥಾ *anthá,* such (remote.)

ಅಂತು *antu,* ಅಂತೂ *antú,* however, at any rate.

ಅಂತೆ *ante,* like, as, such as.

ಅಲ್ಲದೆ *allade,* besides, or, but, else, except, unless.

ಅಲ್ಲವೆ *allave,* or, else.

ಆಗಲೇ *ágalé,* that instant, that very time.

ಆಗಾಗ *ágága,* ಆಗಾಗ್ಯೆ *ágágye* from time to time, gradually.

ಆಗ್ಯೂ *ágyú,* though, notwithstanding.

ಇಂತ *inta,* ಇಂತಲು *intalu,* than, (as an affix.)

ಇಂತ *inta,* ಇಂತಾ *intá,* ಇಂಥ *intha,* ಇಂಥಾ *inthá,* such (proximate.)

ಇಂತು *intu,* ಇಂತೂ *intú,* thus, so.

ಈಗಲೇ *ígalé,* this instant, at this very time.

ಈಗಾಗಿ *ígági,* instantly, just now.

ಉಸಿಕ್ಕನೆ *usikkane,* silently, softly, gently.

ಎಂತ *yenta,* ಎಂತಲು *yentalu,* thus, so, that is.

ಎಂತ *yenta,* ಎಂತಾ *yentá,* ಎಂಥ *yentha,* ಎಂಥಾ *yenthá,* of what kind?

ಎಂತು *yentu,* how?

ಎಂತೂ *yentú,* by all means, somehow or other.

ಎಂದೂ *yendú,* ಎಂದಿಗೂ *yendigú,* ಎಂದೆಂದಿಗೂ *yendendigú,* always, for ever.

ಎಂದಾದರೂ *yendádarú,* at any time, at some time.

ಎಂದು *yendu,* ಎಂಬದಾಗಿ *yembadági,* so saying, (used to mark a quotation of what another has said.)

ಎದುರಾಗಿ *yedurági,* opposite to, in presence of.

ಒಮ್ಮೆ *womme,* once, one time.

ಓಪಾದೆಯಲ್ಲಿ *ópádeyalli,* like, as.

ಕೂಡ್ಲೆ *kúḍle,* immediately, upon that.

ತಿರಿಗಿ *tirigi,* again, once more.

ನೆಟ್ಟಗೆ *neṭṭage,* directly, properly, in a straightforward direction.

ನುಣ್ಣಗೆ *nuṇṇage,* ನುಣ್ಣನೇ *nuṇṇane,* evenly, smoothly.

ಫಕ್ಕನೆ *phakkane,* suddenly.

ಬರಿದೇ *baridé,* merely, in vain.

ಬಹಳ *bahaḷa,* much, many.

ಬಹಳವಾಗಿ *bahaḷawági,* abundantly.

ಬಿರ್ರನೆ *birrane,* quickly.

ಬೆಳಿಗ್ಯೆ *beḷigye,* in the morning.

ಬೇಗ *béga,* ಬೇಗನೆ *bégane,* quickly.

ಮತ್ತು *mattu,* ಮತ್ತೆ *matte,* other, further, more, again, moreover.

ಮುಂಚೆ *munche,* ಮುಂಚಿತವಾಗಿ *munchitawági,* formerly, before, prior, early.

ಮುಖಾಂತರ *mukhántara,* by means of, through.

ಮುಂದಾಗಿ *mundági,* in presence of, in front of.

ಮೆಲ್ಲಗೆ *mellage,* slowly, gently, softly.

ಯಾವಾಗಲೂ *yáwágalú,* always, ever.

ಯಾವಾಗಾದರೂ *yáwágádarú,* ಯಾವಾಗಲಾದರೂ *yáwágaládarú,* at any time, at some time.

ವಿಂಗಡವಾಗಿ *vingaḍawági,* separately, distinctly, apart.

ಶೀಘ್ರವಾಗಿ *shíghrawági,* swiftly.

ಸುಮ್ಮನೆ *summane,* ಸುಮ್ಮಗೆ *summage,* only, merely, in vain, quietly, without object or aim.

ಸಂಗಡಲೇ *sangaḍalé,* immediately.

ಹತ್ತರ *hattara,* ಹತ್ರ *hatra,* near, at hand.

ಹಾಗೆ *háge,* ಹಾಂಗೆ *hánge,* so, in *that* manner, so that, in order that, like as.

ಹಾಗಾದರೂ *hágádarú,* or, at least, even.

ಹೀಗೆ *híge,* ಹೀಂಗೆ *hínge,* thus, in *this* manner.

ಹ್ಯಾಗೆ *hyáge,* ಹ್ಯಾಂಗೆ *hyánge,* how, in what manner?

ಹ್ಯಾಗೂ *hyágú,* ಹ್ಯಾಗಾದರೂ *hyágádarú,* by any means, at any rate.

POSTPOSITIONS. (321.)

140. The following postpositions govern the genitive case of nouns and pronouns.

ಒಡನೆ *woḍane* with, along with. *Adv.* forthwith, directly.

ಕೂಡ *kúḍa,* ಕೂಡಾ *kúḍá,* also, with (not instrumental.)

ಕೆಳಗೆ *keḷage,* beneath, down, under, below.

ತರುವಾಯ *taruváya,* after. *Adv.* afterwards.

ತನಕ *tanaka,* till, until, as far as.

ತೊಸುಕ *tusuka,* for, in order to.

ಪರ್ಯಂತ *paryanta,* ಪರ್ಯಂತರ *paryantara,* until, as far as, up to.

ಬಗ್ಗೆ *bagye,* for, on account of.

ಬಳಿಕ *baḷika,* after, afterwards.

ಮಟ್ಟಿಗೆ *maṭṭige,* till, until, as far as.

ಮುಂದೆ *munde,* before, in presence of.

ಮೇಲೆ *méle,* after, upon, over, above.

ನಿಮಿತ್ತ *nimitta,* ನಿಮಿತ್ತವಾಗಿ *nimittawági,* for, on account of, in order to.

ವರಿಗೆ *varige,* ವರಿಗೂ *varigú,* till, until, as far as.

ಸಂಗಡ *sangaḍa,* ಸಂಗಾತ *sangáta,* along with, in company with.

141. The following govern the dative case. (168—170.)

ಓಸರ *ósara,* ಓಸ್ಕರ *óskara,* ಓಸ್ಕರವಾಗಿ *óskarawági,* for, for the purpose of, in order to, on account of.

ಮುಂಚೆ *munche,* ಮುಂಚಿತವಾಗಿ *munchitawági,* before, as to time. (See adverbs.)

ಹೊರತು *horatu,* ಹೊರ್ತು *hortu,* ಹೊರ್ತಾಗಿ *hortági,* except, besides, without, may follow any case.

142. CONJUNCTIONS. (322—336.)

ಆದರು *ádaru,* ಆದರೂ *ádarú,* (subjunctive of ಆಗು *águ,* Become,) or, even, any, at least, though.

ಆದರೆ *ádare,* (subjunctive of ಆಗು *águ,*) but, if, supposing it be so.

ಆಗಲಿ *ágali,* (Imperative of ಆಗು *águ,*) let it be, be it so, either, or.

ಆದಾಗ್ಯೂ *ádágyú,* however, notwithstanding, even, though.

ಆದ್ದರಿಂದ *áddarinda,* ಆದದರಿಂದ *ádadarinda,* therefore, because.

ಇನ್ನೂ *innú,* more, yet, still.

ಅಲ್ಲದೆ *allade,*
ಅಲ್ಲವೆ *allave,* } or, but, besides. (See postpositions.)

ಊ *ú,* (in composition,) and, also, even.

ಏನೋ *yénó,* (in composition,) whether it is or not, Is it so or not.

ಸಹ *saha,* with, even, also.

ಊ ಇಲ್ಲ *ú illa,* ಊ ಅಲ್ಲ *ú alla,* (if repeated,) neither, nor.

143. INTERJECTIONS.

ಅಯ್ಯೋ *ayyó*,
ಅಕಟಾ *akaṭá*,
ಕುಯ್ಯೋ *kuyyó*,
ಮೊರ್ರೋ *morró*,
} expressive of sorrow and pain.

ಅಃ *ah*,
ಆಃ *áh*,
ಅಹಹ *ahaha*,
} expressive of surprise, pleasure, admiration, jest, or reproach.

ಎಲೆ *yele*,
ಎಲೇ *yelé*,
ಎಲೆಗೆ *yelege*,
ಎಲೈ *yelei*,
ಎಲಾ *yelá*,
ಎಲೋ *yeló*,
ಓ *ó*,
} O! oh!

ಛೀ *chhí*, ಇಸ್ *is*, expressive of disgust.
ಅಶಿಶಿ *ashishi*, expressive of dissent, dislike.

144. PARTICLES. (337, 338.)

ಆ *á*, ಏ *é*, ಓ *ó*, and ಏನೋ *yénó*, denote doubt, question or interrogation.
ಏ *é*, an emphatic particle denoting affirmation.
ಊ *ú*, and, also, even.
ರೆ *re*, if.
ಕಾಣೆ *káṇe*, (fem.)
ಕಾಣೋ *káṇó*, (mas.)
} are sometimes added to ಹೌದು *houdu*, yes, when addressing inferiors.

SYNTAX.

ARTICLES.

145. There are no Articles in Canarese. The best substitutes for the Indefinite Article are, ಒಂದು *wondu*, one (thing,) and ಒಬ್ಬ *wobba*, one (person.)

146. The place of the Definite Article is supplied by the abbreviated Demonstrative pronouns ಆ *á* that, and ಈ *í*, this.

CASES OF NOUNS. (46.)

147. The Nominative case precedes the verb ; as,
ಗುರುವು ಹೇಳಿದನು *guruvu héḷidanu*, The priest said.
ಅವರು ಹೋದರು *avaru hódaru*, They went.

148. The crude form of the noun is often used for the Nominative case; as,
ಗುರು ಹೇಳಿದನು *guru héḷidanu*, The priest said.
ಮರ ಬಿತ್ತು *mara bittu*, The tree fell.

ACCUSATIVE CASE.

149. The Accusative case precedes the verb which governs it. The usual order is, 1st, the nominative case, 2nd, the accusative, and 3rd, the active verb; as, ಅರಸನು ರಾಜ್ಯವನ್ನು ಆಳಿದನು *arasanu rájyavannu áḷidanu*, The king governed the country.

150. The crude form of the noun is often used for the accusative. In such case the final vowel is generally lengthened; as, ಅನ್ನಾ (ಅನ್ನವನ್ನು) ತಿಂದನು *anná tindanu*, He ate rice.

INSTRUMENTAL CASE.

151. The Instrumental case is used, First, as the agent of passive verbs; as, ಅರಸನಿಂದ ಜನರು ರಕ್ಷಿಸಲ್ಪಟ್ಟರು *arasaninda janaru rakṣhisalpaṭṭaru*, The people were protected by the king.

152. Second, to express the cause or instrument of an action; as,
ಬೆಂಕಿಯಿಂದ ಮರ ಸುಟ್ಟು ಹೋಯಿತು *benkiyinda mara suṭṭu hóyitu*, The wood was consumed by fire.
ಕತ್ತಿಯಿಂದ ಅವನನ್ನು ಕೊಂದು ಹಾಕಿದನು *kattiyinda avanannu kondu-hákidanu*, He killed him with a sword.

153. Third, to express the material of which a thing is composed; as, ಮಣ್ಣಿನಿಂದ ಕಟ್ಟಿದ ಗೋಡೆ *maṇṇininda kaṭṭida góḍe*, A wall built of mud.

154. Fourth, to denote motion from; as, ಮನೆಯಿಂದ ಹೊರಟನು *muneyinda horaṭanu*, He went out of the house.

ಕಚೇರಿಯಿಂದ ಬಂತು *kachériyinda bantu*, It came from the cutcherry.

155. Fifth, it is sometimes used to express comparison; as, ಅದರಿಂದ ದೊಡ್ಡದು *adarinda doḍḍadu*, Bigger than that.

DATIVE CASE.

156. The dative case is used, First, when the act of giving is expressed; as, ನನಗೆ ಪುಸ್ತಕ ಕೊಡು *nanage pustaka koḍu*, Give me a book.

157. Second, in denoting motion towards; as, ಅವನ ಬಳಿಗೆ ಹೋಗು *avana baḷige hógu*, Go to him.

ತುಮ್ಮುಕೂರಿಗೆ ಶೇರಿದರು *tummukúrige shéridaru*, They arrived at Toomkoor.

158. Third, in expressing the distance between two places. Sometimes one, but generally both places are put in the Dative case; as, ಬೆಂಗಳೂರಿಗೂ ಮೈಸೂರಿಗೂ ಎಷ್ಟು ದೂರ *bengaḷúrigú meisúrigú yeshṭu dúra*, What is the distance between Bangalore and Mysore?

159. Fourth, in pointing out relative position; as,

ಆ ದೇಶ ಈ ದೇಶಕ್ಕೆ ದೂರವಾಗಿದೆ *á désha í déshakke dúravágide*, That country is distant from this.

ಆ ದೇಶ ಈ ದೇಶಕ್ಕೆ ಉತ್ತರ ಕಡೆಯಲ್ಲಿ ಅದೆ *á désha í déshakke uttara kaḍeyalli ade*, That country is to the north of this.

ಅದಕ್ಕೆ ಆಚೆ *adakke áche*, Beyond that.

160. Fifth, in denoting property or possession; as,

ಅವನಿಗೆ ಬಹಳ ಕೋಪ ಉಂಟು *avanige bahaḷa kópa unṭu*, He is very angry.

ನನಗೆ ಬಹಳ ಆಶೆ ಉಂಟು *nanage bahaḷa áshe unṭu*, I have great desire.

ನಿಮಗೆ ಐಶ್ವರ್ಯವಿಲ್ಲವೋ *nimage eishvaryavillavó*, Have you not wealth?

161. Sixth, in comparing; as,

ಅದಕ್ಕೂ ಇದಕ್ಕೂ ಬಹು ಹೆಚ್ಚುಕಡಿಮೆ *adakkú idakkú bahu hechchu kaḍime*, There is a great difference betwixt that and this.

ನಿನಗೆ ನಾನು ಕಡೆಯೋ *ninage nánu kaḍeyó*, Am I baser than thou?

ನೀನು ಎಲ್ಲರಿಗೂ ಗರ್ವಿಷ್ಠನು *nínu yellarigú garvishṭhanu*, You are prouder than all.

162. Seventh, in stating relationship; as, ನಿನಗೆ ಅವನು ತಮ್ಮನೋ *ninage avanu tammanó*, Is he your younger brother?

163. Eighth, in expressing end or purpose; as,

ಯಾತಕ್ಕೆ ಬಂದೆ *yátakke bande*, Why have you come?

ಕೆಲಸಕ್ಕೆ ಬಂದೆ *kelasakke bande*, I came on business.

ನೋಡುವದಕ್ಕೆ ಹೋದೆನು *nóḍuvadakke hódenu,* I went to see.

164. Ninth, in denoting exchange; as,

ಎಷ್ಟಕ್ಕೆ ಕೊಡುತ್ತೀರಿ *yeshṭakke koḍuttíri,* For how much will you give it?

ಎರಡು ರೂಪಾಯಿಗೆ ಕೊಡುತ್ತೇನೆ *yeraḍu rúpáyige koḍutténe,* I will give it for two rupees.

165. Tenth, in expressing time; as,

ಇಂದಿಗೆ *indige,* To day.

ಸಾಯಂಕಾಲಕ್ಕೆ *sáyankálakke,* In the evening.

ಎರಡು ವರುಷಕ್ಕೆ *yeraḍu varushakke,* For two years.

ಈ ತಿಂಗಳಿಗೆ ಆರು ತಿಂಗಳು *í tingaḷige áru tingaḷu,* Six months this month.

166. Eleventh, with many verbs; as,

ನನಗೆ ತಿಳಿಯದು *nanage tiḷiyadu,* I know not.

ಅವನಿಗೆ ಹುಚ್ಚು ಹಿಡಿಯಿತು *avanige huchchu hiḍiyitu,* He went mad.

ನಿಮಗೆ ಶಿಕ್ಕಿತೋ *nimage shikkitó,* Have you found it?

ಅದಕ್ಕೆ ಹೆದರಿ ಕೊಂಡೆನು *adakke hedari koṇḍenu,* I was terrified at (or by) it; &c. &c.

167. Twelfth, when followed by certain postpositions; as,

ಆ ದಿವಸಕ್ಕೆ ಮುಂಚೆ *á divasakke munche,* Before that day.

ಇದಕ್ಕೋಸ್ಕರ *idakkóskara,* For this purpose.

168. Thirteenth, in expressing liability or exposure to, worthiness of, &c.; as,

ನರಕಕ್ಕೆ ಗುರಿಯಾಗಿದ್ಧಾನೆ *narakakke guriyágiddháne,* He is in danger of (exposed to) hell.

ದಯಕ್ಕೆ ಪಾತ್ರನು *dayakke pátranu,* Worthy of kindness; a fit object of favour.

169. Fourteenth, in nearly all cases represented in English by *to, for,* &c.

ABLATIVE CASE.

171. This case is formed by adding the instrumental case of the word ದೆಸೆ *dese,* to the genitive of other nouns. It is not in frequent use. It is generally used interchangeably with the instrumental case, but in certain positions conveys a slightly different meaning.

172. Its signification may be represented by *from, away from, off from,* &c.; as,

ಮರದದೆಸೆಯಿಂದ ಹಣ್ಣು ಬಿತ್ತು *marada-deseyinda haṇṇu bittu,* The fruit fell *down from* the tree.

GENITIVE CASE.

173. The Genitive case is used to denote relation, connexion or possession; as,

ಹಸುವಿನ ಹಾಲು *hasuvina hálu*, Cow's milk.

ಪಟ್ಣದ ಗೋಡೆ *paṭṇada góḍe*, The city wall.

ಅವರ ನೆಂಟರು *avara neṇṭaru*, Their relatives.

174. Frequently the form of the genitive case is put for the accusative; as,

ಅವನ ಹೊಡೆದರು *avana hoḍedaru*, They beat him.

175. Many postpositions govern the genitive case of nouns and pronouns to which they are affixed; as the following examples shew:—

ಅಂತೆ *ante*, like; as, ಅವಳಂತೆ *avaḷante*, Like her.

176. ಒಡನೆ *oḍane*, with; as,

ನನ್ನೊಡನೆ *nannoḍane*, With me.

ಅವರೊಡನೆ *avaroḍane*, With them.

177. ಓಪಾದೆಯಲ್ಲಿ *ópádeyalli*, like; as,

ಅದರೋಪಾದೆಯಲ್ಲಿ *adarópádeyalli*, Like that.

ಪುಸ್ತಕದೋಪಾದೆಯಲ್ಲಿ *pustakadópádeyalli*, Like a book.

178. ಕೂಡ *kúḍa*, With, along with; as, ನನ್ನ ಕೂಡ ಹೋಗುತ್ತೀಯಾ *nanna kúḍa hóguttíyá*, Will you accompany me?

179. ಕೆಳಗೆ *keḷage*, under, below; as, ಭೂಮಿಯ ಕೆಳಗೆ *bhúmiya keḷage*, Under the earth.

180. ತರುವಾಯ *taruwáya*, after; as, ಅದರ ತರುವಾಯ ಏನಾಯಿತು *adara taruwáya yénáyitu*, What happened after that?

181. ತನಕ *tanaka*, till, until, as far as; as, ಆರು ತಿಂಗಳುಗಳ ತನಕ *áru tingaḷugaḷa tanaka*, Till six months.

182. ತುಸುಕ *tusuka*, ತುಸುಕಾಗಿ *tusukági*, for, on account of; as, ಇದರ ತುಸುಕ *idara tusuka*, On this account.

183. ಪರ್ಯಂತರ *paryantara*, till, until, as far as; as, ನಾಲ್ಕು ದಿವಸದ ಪರ್ಯಂತರ *nálku divasada paryantara*, Till four days.

184. ಬಗ್ಯೆ *bagye*, for, on account of; as, ಆ ಕೆಲಸದ ಬಗ್ಯೆ *á kelasada bagye*, On account of that work.

185. ಬಳಿಕ *baḷika*, afterwards; as, ಅದರ ಬಳಿಕ *adara baḷika*, After that.

186. ಮಟ್ಟಿಗೆ *maṭṭige*, till, as far as; as, ಅವನ ಮಟ್ಟಿಗೆ *avana maṭṭige*, To the extent of his ability.

187. ಮೇಲೆ *méle*, upon, above, after; as,

ಮೇಜಿನ ಮೇಲೆ *méjina méle*, Upon the table.

ಹೊಸಕೋಟೆಯ ಮೇಲೆ ಕೋಲಾರಕ್ಕೆ ಹೋದೆವು *hosakóteya méle kólárakke hódevu,* We went by way of Oscotta to Colar.

ಅದರ ಮೇಲೆ *adara méle,* Upon (above, or after) that.

188. ನಿಮಿತ್ತ *nimitta,* ನಿಮಿತ್ತವಾಗಿ *nimittawági,* on account of; as,

ಕೆಲಸದ ನಿಮಿತ್ತ ಬಂದರು *kelasada nimitta bandaru,* They came on business.

189. ವರಿಗೆ *varige,* until, as far as; as,

ಈ ದಿನದ ವರಿಗೆ *í dinada varige,* Till this day.

190. ಸುತ್ತ *sutta,* ಸುತ್ತಲು *suttalu,* about, around; as,

ಪಟ್ಣದ ಸುತ್ತ *paṭṇada sutta,* Around the city.

191. ಸಂಗಡ *sangaḍa,* ಸಂಗಾತ *sangáta,* with, along with; as,

ಅವರ ಸಂಗಡ ಹೋಗು *avara sangaḍa hógu,* Go with them.

192. ಹತ್ತರ *hattara,* by, close to, near, with; as,

ಧೊರೆಯ ಹತ್ತರ ಹೋದರು *dhoreya hattara hódaru,* They went to the king.

ನನ್ನ ಹತ್ತರ ದುಡ್ಡಿಲ್ಲ *nanna hattara duḍḍilla,* I have no money by me.

193. ಹೊರಗೆ *horage,* without; as,

ಪಟ್ಣದ ಹೊರಗೆ *paṭṇada horage,* Without the city.

LOCATIVE CASE.

194. The Locative case is used, First, to express situation; as,

ಮನೆಯಲ್ಲಿ ಇದ್ದನು *maneyalli iddanu,* He was in the house.

ಅವರು ಊರಲ್ಲಿ ಇಲ್ಲವೋ *avaru úralli illavó,* Are they not in the town?

ಪೆಟ್ಟಿಗೆಯಲ್ಲಿ ಶಿಕ್ಕಿತು *peṭṭigeyalli shikkitu,* It was found in the box.

195. Second, to denote possession; as,

ನಿಮ್ಮಲ್ಲಿ ಹಣ ಉಂಟೋ *nimmalli haṇa uṇṭó,* Have you any money?

196. Third, to form degrees of comparison; as,

ಆ ಇಬ್ಬರಲ್ಲಿ ಇವನೇ ವಿವೇಕಿ *á ibbaralli ivané rivéki,* This man is the wiser of the two.

ಅವನು ಎಲ್ಲರಲ್ಲಿ ಶ್ರೇಷ್ಠನು *avanu yellaralli shréṣhṭhanu,* He is the greatest of all.

ಯುದ್ಧದಲ್ಲಿ ಸಮರ್ಥನು *yuddhadalli samarthanu,* A mighty man in battle.

197. Fourth, to denote the instrument of an action, or the material of which a thing is made; as,

ಕೋಲಿನಲ್ಲಿ ಹೊಡೆದನು *kólinalli hoḍedanu,* He beat with a stick.

ಮರದಲ್ಲಿ ಮಾಡಿದ್ದು *maradalli máḍiddu,* Made of wood.

ಸುಣ್ಣದಲ್ಲಿ ಕಟ್ಟಿದ್ದು *suṇṇadalli kaṭṭiddu,* Built with lime.

N. B. To denote motion from out of, the affix of the instrumental case is added to the locative; as,

ಅವರಲ್ಲಿಂದ ಹೊರಟು ಬಂದನು *avarallinda horaṭu bandanu*, He came out from among them.

ಪಟ್ಣದಲ್ಲಿಂದ ಜನರು ಓಡಿ ಹೋದರು *paṭṇadallinda janaru wóḍi hódaru*, The people ran out of the city.

VOCATIVE CASE.

198. The Vocative case is generally formed as shewn in the Declensions of Nouns, by lengthening the final vowel of the nominative, or adding ಏ *é*, to the nominative; as,

ಗಜಾ *gajá*, or ಗಜವೇ *gajavé*, O elephant.
ಮರಾ *mará*, or ಮರವೇ *maravé*, O tree.
ಗುರುವೇ *guruvé*, O priest.

But in addition to these, the vocative particles, ಆ *á*, ಓ *ó*, ಎಲೇ *yelé*, &c. are often prefixed to nouns without distinction of sex or rank.

ಅಣೇ *aṇé*, and ಎಲೆಗೇ *yelegé*, are used in calling a female.
ಎಲೈ *yelei*, is used in addressing a superior.
ಎಲಾ *yelá*, ಎಲೋ *yeló*, in addressing an inferior.

199. In prose compositions, the vocative case generally, but not always, begins the sentence; as,

ಜನರೇ ಕೇಳಿರಿ *janaré kéḷiri*, Here, O people.
ಅಪ್ಪಾ ಈ ಕೆಲಸಾ ಮಾಡು *appá í kelasá máḍu*, Sir, do this work.
ಎಲ್ಲಿಗೆ ಹೋಗುತ್ತೀರಯ್ಯಾ *yellige hóguttírayyá*, Where are you going, sir?

In poetry the situation of the vocative is a matter of choice or convenience; as,

ನೆಚ್ಚನಯ್ಯಾ ಹರಿಯೊಪ್ಪನಯ್ಯಾ *nechchan ayyá, hari oppan ayyá*, He will not believe, Sir; Hari will not approve, Sir.

ದಾರಿ ಯೇನಿದಕ್ಕೆ ಮುರಾರೀ ನೀ ಕೈ ಹಿಡಿಯದಿದ್ದರೆ *dári yén idakke, murárí, ní kei hiḍiyadiddare*, How can I accomplish this, O Murári, except you aid me?

200. The repetition of a noun or pronoun expresses *each*, *abundance*, and *excess* in degree, quality, or quantity; as,

ಅವನವನಿಗೆ ಒಂದೊಂದು ರೂಪಾಯಿ ಕೊಡು *avanavanige wondondu rúpáyi koḍu*, Give a rupee to each.

ದಿನದಿನಕ್ಕೆ *dinadinakke*, Day by day; every day.
ವರುಷವರುಷಕ್ಕೆ *varuṣha varuṣhakke*, Year by year.

201. Sometimes ಆಗಿ *ági*, is added to the repeated word; as,

ಮುಳ್ಳು ಮುಳ್ಳಾಗಿ *muḷḷu muḷḷági*, Thorny; full of thorns.
ಗುಂಪು ಗುಂಪಾಗಿ *gumpu gumpági*, In crowds.

ADJECTIVES.

202. The Adjective precedes the noun of which it expresses the quality; as,

ದೊಡ್ಡ ಊರು *doḍḍa úru*, A large town.

ಬಿಳಿ ಕುದುರೆ *biḷi kudure*, A white horse.

But a noun of quality, that is, an adjective with a personal termination, follows the noun or pronoun with which it is connected; as,

ಅವನು ಒಳ್ಳೆಯವನು *avanu woḷḷeyavanu*, He is a good man.

ಅವಳು ಕೆಟ್ಟವಳು *avaḷu keṭṭavaḷu*, She is a bad woman.

203. The repetition of an adjective denotes excess in degree or quality; as,

ಚಿಕ್ಕ ಚಿಕ್ಕ ಹಕ್ಕಿಗಳು *chikka chikka hakkigaḷu*, Very little birds.

ಕೊಂಚ ಕೊಂಚ ಹುಲ್ಲು *koncha koncha hullu*, A very little grass.

ದೊಡ್ಡ ದೊಡ್ಡ ಪಟ್ಣ *doḍḍa doḍḍa paṭṇa*, A very large city.

PERSONAL PRONOUNS.

204. The crude state of pronouns is sometimes used for the nominative case; as,

ನಾ ಕಾಣೆ *ná káṇe*, I dont know.

ನೀ ಹೋದಿಯಾ *ní hódiyá*, Did you go?

ಅವ ಒಳ್ಳೆಯವ *ava woḷḷeyava*, He is a good man.

ಈತ ಬಲ್ಲ *íta balla*, This man knows.

205. Relation or possession is expressed by adding pronouns of the third person to the genitive of nouns and pronouns; as,

ಅವನು ನನ್ನವನು *avanu nannavanu*, He is mine.

ಇವಳು ನಿನ್ನವಳೋ *ivaḷu ninnavaḷó*, Does this woman belong to you?

ಆ ಪುಸ್ತಕ ನನ್ನದಲ್ಲ *á pustaka nannadalla*, That book is not mine.

ಈ ಎತ್ತು ಯಾರದು *í yettu yáradu*, Whose ox is this?

ಆ ಕುರಿಗಳು ನಿನ್ನವೋ *á kurigaḷu ninnavó*, Are those sheep yours?

206. The plurals ನಾವು *návu*, we, and ನೀವು *nívu*, ye, are very commonly used in the singular, when a person of respectability speaks of himself, or to an equal or superior; as,

ನಾವು ಮಾಡಲಿಲ್ಲ *návu máḍalilla*, I did not do.

ನೀವು ದಯಮಾಡಿ ಬರ ಬೇಕು *nívu daya máḍi bara béku*, You (sing.) must be pleased to come.

207. The singular ನೀನು *nínu,* Thou, is disrespectful except when addressing inferiors.

208. In addressing persons of very superior rank, the reciprocal pronoun ತಾವು *távu,* themselves, is used for the second person singular ; as,

ತಾವು ಯಾವಾಗ ದಯ ಮಾಡಿದಿರಿ *távu yáwága daya mádidiri,* When did you (singular) arrive ? (*lit.* favour us.)

DEMONSTRATIVE PRONOUNS.

209. The singular ಅವನು *avanu,* he, and ಅವಳು *avaḷu,* she, are used when speaking of an equal or inferior. The plural ಅವರು *avaru,* they, is used as an honorific singular when speaking of a superior.

210. ಆತನು *átanu,* he, ಆಕೆಯು *ákeyu,* she, with their proximates, ಈತನು *ítanu,* he, ಈಕೆಯು *íkeyu,* she, are used of an equal or superior when respect is intended.

RECIPROCAL PRONOUN.

211. ತಾನು *tánu,* himself, herself, itself, is used with reference to a preceding nominative of the third person, expressed or understood ; as,

ವರ್ತಕನು ತನ್ನ ಮನೆಗೆ ಹೋದನು *wartakanu tanna manege hódanu,* The merchant went to his house.

ಅವಳು ತನ್ನ ಎದೆ ಬಡುಕೊಂಡಳು *avaḷu tanna yede baḍukoṇḍaḷu,* She beat her breast.

ಆನೆ ಅವನನ್ನು ತನ್ನ ಕಾಲಿನಿಂದ ತುಳಿಯಿತು *áne avanannu tanna kálininda tuḷiyitu,* The elephant trampled him with its foot.

ಜನರೆಲ್ಲರು ತಮ್ಮ ತಮ್ಮ ಊರುಗಳಿಗೆ ಹೋದರು *janarellaru tamma tamma úrugaḷige hódaru,* All the people went to their several towns.

ತನ್ನ ಬಾಯಿ ತೆರೆಯಿತು *tanna báyi tereyitu,* It opened its mouth.

ತಾವು ಕೋರಿದ ಹಾಗೆ ಮಾಡಿದರು *távu kórida háge máḍidaru,* They did as they wished.

In the last two examples the nominative is understood.

212. The plural, ತಾವು *távu,* themselves, is used as a second person singular, in shewing the highest respect ; and is equivalent to "your honor," "your Lordship," &c ; as,

ತಮಗೆ ತಿಳಿದಿರ ಬೇಕು *tamage tiḷidira béku,* Your honor must be aware.

ತಮ್ಮ ಕಟಾಕ್ಷದಿಂದ ಬದುಕುತ್ತೇನೆ *tamma kaṭákshadinda badukutténe,* I live by your lordship's favour.

ತಾವು ನನ್ನ ಮನವಿಯನ್ನು ಚಿತ್ತೈಸ ಬೇಕು *távu nanna manaviyannu chitteisa béku,* I beg your lordship to consider my request.

INTERROGATIVE PRONOUNS.

213. The singular ಯಾವನು *yávanu,* and ಯಾವಳು *yávaḷu,* are seldom used alone. The plural form ಯಾರು *yáru,* who, is used also for the singular of the masculine and feminine genders; as,

ನೀನು ಯಾರು *nínu yáru,* Who are you?

ಇವನು ಯಾರು *ivanu yáru,* Who is this man?

ಅವಳು ಯಾರು *avaḷu yáru,* Who is she?

ಇದನ್ನು ಮಾಡಿದವರು ಯಾರು *idannu máḍidavaru yáru,* Who are they who did this?

ಅಲ್ಲಿ ನಿಂತಿರುವ ಹೆಂಗಸರು ಯಾರು *alli nintiruva hengasaru yáru,* Who are those women standing there?

ಯಾರು *yáru,* is used also with the singular neuter in the expression ಅದು ಯಾರು *adu yáru,* Who is that? or, who is there?

214. The crude form ಯಾವ *yáva,* is used with all the genders, and with both numbers; as,

ಯಾವ ಧೊರೆ *yáva dhore,* What king?

ಯಾವ ಸ್ತ್ರೀ *yáva strí,* What woman?

ಯಾವ ಗ್ರಂಥ *yáva grantha,* What book?

ಯಾವ ಜನರು *yáva janaru,* What people?

ಯಾವ ಹೆಂಗಸರು *yáva hengasaru,* What women?

ಯಾವ ಸ್ಥಳಗಳಲ್ಲಿ *yáva sthaḷagaḷalli,* In what places?

215. When two or more pronouns of different *persons* are used together in a sentence, if one of them be of the First person, the verb and pronoun which refer to them must be of the first person plural; as,

ಅವನೂ ನೀನೂ ನಾನೂ ಅಲ್ಲಿ ಇದ್ದೆವು ಮತ್ತು ನಾವು ನಡೆದದ್ದೆಲ್ಲಾ ನೋಡಿದೆವು *avanú nínú nánú alli iddevu, mattu návu naḍedaddellá nóḍidevu,* He, thou and I were there, and we saw all that took place.

216. If the nominatives be of the Second and Third persons, the verb and pronoun which refer to them must be in the second person plural; as,

ಆ ಮನುಷ್ಯನೂ ನೀನೂ ಕೂಡ ಇದ್ದಿರಿ ಆದರೆ ಏನು ಮಾಡುತ್ತಿದ್ದಿರೋ ನನಗೆ ತಿಳಿಯದು *á manushyanú nínú kúḍa iddiri ádare yénu máḍuttiddiró nanage tiḷiyadu,* That man and you were together, but what you were doing I know not.

VERBS.

217. The verb must agree with its nominative case in gender, number and person; as, ನಾನು ಹೇಳಿದೆನು *nánu hêḷidenu,* I said.

ನೀನು ಕರೆದಿ *nínu karedi,* Thou calledst.

ಅರಸನು ಆಳಿದನು *arasanu áḷidanu,* The king reigned.

ಅವರು ಬಂದಾರು *avaru bandáru,* They will probably come.

218. When the nominative is a collective neuter noun, the verb is frequently put in the singular number, even though the noun has the plural form; as, ದನಗಳು ಬಂತು *danagaḷu bantu,* The cattle came.

219. When there are several nominatives of different genders, if one of the nominatives be masculine, the verb will be masculine, but may agree with the last nominative; as,

ಅರಸೂ ಅರಸಿಯೂ ಆನೆಯೂ ಬಂದರು (or ಬಂದವು) *arasú arasiyú áneyú bandaru,* (or *bandavu,*) The king, the quèen and the elephant came.

But such mixed sentences are very rare.

220. If the nominative consist of two or more personal pronouns, and one of them be of the first person, the verb must be of the first person plural; as,

ಅವನೂ ನೀನೂ ನಾನೂ ಮೈಸೂರಿಗೆ ಹೋದೆವು *avanú nínú nánú meisúrige hôdevu,* He, thou and I went to Mysore.

221. When the nominative is a personal pronoun, it is often omitted, the person being determined by the termination of the verb; as,

ಓದುತ್ತೇನೆ *wóduttêne,* I read.

ನೋಡಿದಿಯಾ *nôḍidiyá,* Sawest thou?

ಹೇಳುವಳು *hêḷuvaḷu,* She will say.

ಮಾಡರು *máḍaru,* They will not do.

222. In colloquial speech the termination ನು *nu,* is frequently dropped, except in the second future tense; as, ಬಂದೆ *bande,* I came.

ಸಿಕ್ಕಿದ *shikkida,* He was caught. ಹಾಡುವೆ *háḍuve,* I will sing.

GERUNDS.

223. The gerund may be regarded as a suspensive tense, as its person, gender and time are determined by the final verb, except where the nominative is expressed. It is used in relating a series of actions.

224. In expressing simultaneous or nearly connected actions, the *present* gerund is used; as,

ಹಾಡುತ್ತಾ ಬಂದನು *háḍuttá bandanu,* He came singing.

ಹುಡುಗರು ತೋಟದಲ್ಲಿ ತಿರುಗಾಡುತ್ತಾ, ಮರಗಳನ್ನು ಹತ್ತುತ್ತಾ, ಹಣ್ಣು ತಿನ್ನುತ್ತಾ, ಒಬ್ಬರನ್ನೊಬ್ಬರು ಕೂಗುತ್ತಾ ಹೆಸರು ಹಿಡಿದು ಕರೆಯುತ್ತಾ, ನಗುತ್ತಾ, ಆಡುತ್ತಾ ಇದ್ದರು *huḍugaru tóṭadalli tirugáḍuttá, maragaḷannu hattuttá, haṇṇu tinnuttá, wobbarannobbaru kúguttá, hesaru hiḍidu kareyuttá, naguttá, áḍuttá iddaru,* The boys were rambling about the garden, climbing the trees, eating fruit, shouting to each other, calling each other by name, laughing and playing.

If instead of ಇದ್ದರು *iddaru,* the final verb be in the present tense, ಇದ್ದಾರೆ *iddhárе,* the whole of the actions become present, and the sentence would read, "The boys *are,*" &c.

If the future ಇರುವರು *iruvaru,* be used, the whole sentence is future, and would read, "The boys *will be,*" &c. &c.

225. In relating a series of successive actions, the *Past* gerund is used; as,

ಹೊಲಕ್ಕೆ ಹೋಗಿ, ಹುಲ್ಲು ಕೊಯಿದು, ಹೊರೆ ಕಟ್ಟಿ, ಎತ್ತುಗಳ ಹಿಡಿದು ಕೊಂಡು, ಮನೆಗೆ ಬಂದೆನು *holakke hógi, hullu koidu, hore kaṭṭi, yettugaḷa hiḍidu koṇḍu, manege bandenu,* I went to the field, cut grass, tied it up in a bundle, took the oxen, and came home.

If the final verb be ಬರುವೆನು *baruvenu,* the whole of the actions will be future, and the sentence read, "I will go," &c.

If the final verb be of any other number or person, the whole sentence will be altered accordingly. Thus,

If ಬಂದೆವು *bandevu,* be used, it will read, "*We went,*" &c.

If ಬಂದಳು *bandaḷu,* "She went," &c.

If ಬರುವರು *baruvaru,* "*They will* go," &c.

226. When negative actions are related, the negative gerund is used; as, ಮಠಕ್ಕೆ ಹೋಗದೆ, ಓದದೆ, ಬರೆಯದೆ, ಪಾಠ ಒಪ್ಪಿಸದೆ, ಏನೂ ಕಲಿಯದೆ, ಆ ಹುಡುಗನು ಧಡ್ಡನಾದನು *maṭhakke hógade, wódade, bareyade, páṭhu woppisade, yénú kaliyade, á huḍuganu dhaḍḍanádanu,* That boy by not going to school, nor reading, nor writing, nor saying lessons, learnt nothing, and became a dunce.

227. The repetition of the gerund denotes progress or continuance; as, ನಡೆಯುತ್ತಾ ನಡೆಯುತ್ತಾ ಊರಿಗೆ ಸೇರಿದರು *naḍeyuttá, naḍeyuttá úrige shéridaru,* By continuing to proceed they reached the village.

ನಾನು ಅವನನ್ನು ಕೇಳಿ ಕೇಳಿ ಸಾಕಾಯಿತು *nánu avanannu kéḷi kéḷi sákáyitu,* I am tired of asking him.

228. The past and negative gerunds sometimes express a cause; as,

ಓದಿ ಓದಿ ಮರುಳಾದ *wódi wódi maruḷáda,* He became crazed by study.

ಏನೂ ಓದದೆ ಧಡ್ಡನಾದನು *yénú wódade dhaḍḍanádanu,* By not studying any thing he became a blockhead.

229. The gerunds may have their own nominatives; as,

ಇನ್ನು ನಾಲ್ಕು ದಿವಸ ಇರುತ್ತಲು ಅವನು ಬಂದನು *innu nálku divasa iruttalu avanu bandanu,* He came four days before the time.

ಅವನು ಸತ್ತು ಇಪ್ಪತ್ತು ವರುಷವಾಯಿತು *avanu sattu ippattu varuṣhavâyitu,* It is twenty years since he died.

230. The gerunds are often used in the formation of compound tenses. (See conjugations of verbs.)

231. They are used also in forming compound verbs. (See 280, 281, 283, 291, 293—296, 299, 302.)

RELATIVE PARTICIPLES.

232. Relative participles admit of a nominative case before them, and perform the office of verb and relative pronoun to nouns and pronouns following them; as,

ಅವನು ಮಾಡಿದ ಕೆಲಸ *avanu máḍida kelasa,* The work which he did.

ನಾವು ಬಂದ ದಾರಿ *návu banda dári,* The way by which we came.

ನೀವು ಹೋಗುವ ಊರು *nívu hóguva úru,* The town to which you are going.

ಕುರಿಗಳು ಇದ್ದ ಹಟ್ಟಿ *kurigaḷu idda haṭṭi,* The fold in which the sheep were.

233. These relative participles may also govern a preceding noun like a verb; as,

ಮನೆಯನ್ನು ಕಟ್ಟಿದ ಮನುಷ್ಯನು *maneyannu kaṭṭida manuṣhyanu,* The man who built the house.

ಕುರಿಗಳನ್ನು ಕಾಯುವ ಕುರುಬನು *kurigaḷannu káyuva kurubanu,* The shepherd who tends sheep.

234. The passive participle requires the instrumental case of the agent or instrument; as,

ಧೊರೆಯಿಂದ ಕೊಡಲ್ಪಟ್ಟ ಭೂಮಿ *dhoreyinda koḍalpaṭṭa bhúmi,* Land given by the king.

ಕೊಡಲಿಯಿಂದ ಕಡಿಯಲ್ಪಟ್ಟ ಮರ *koḍaliyinda kaḍiyalpaṭṭa mara,* The tree which was cut down with an axe.

235. The participles of an intransitive verb are both preceded and followed by nominatives; as,

ನಾನು ಇರುವ ಮನೆ *nánu iruva mane,* The house in which I reside.

ಅವರು ಹೋಗುವ ಪಟ್ಟಣ *avaru hóguva paṭṭaṇa,* The city to which they are going.

ಅವಳು ಬಿದ್ದ ಭಾವಿ *avaḷu bidda bhávi,* The well into which she fell.

236. The relation expressed by the relative participle must often, according to the sense of the verb, be rendered in English by "in which," "from which," "with whom," &c, &c.; as,

ಕಳ್ಳನು ಶಿಕ್ಕಿದ ತಾವು *kaḷḷanu shikkida távu,* The place where (or in which,) the thief was caught.

ದವಸ ಬಂದ ಊರು *davasa banda úru,* The town from which (or to which,) the grain came.

237. Sometimes the relative participle has both a preceding and following nominative, and governs an accusative or other case; as,

ಹುಲಿಯು ಎತ್ತನ್ನು ಕಚ್ಚಿದ ಹಲ್ಲು *huliyu yettannu kachchida hallu,* The tooth with which the tiger bit the ox.

ತಂದೆ ನನಗೆ ಕೊಟ್ಟ ಹಣ *tande nanage koṭṭa haṇa,* The money which my father gave to me.

ನೀನು ಅವನನ್ನು ಕರೆದ ಹೆಸರು *nínu avanannu kareda hesaru,* The name by which you called him.

In such sentences this order is followed; viz. 1st the agent in the nominative case, 2nd the object in the accusative, 3rd the relative participle; and 4th the instrument, &c., in the nominative.

238. Relative participles become nouns by the addition of pronouns, according to the rules of sandhi; as,

ಹೇಳುವ *héḷuva,* who or which says, ಹೇಳುವವನು *héḷuvavanu,* he who says, ಹೇಳುವವಳು *héḷuvavaḷu,* she who says, &c.

ಹೇಳಿದ *héḷida,* who or which said, ಹೇಳಿದವನು *héḷidavanu,* he who said, ಹೇಳಿದವರು *héḷidavaru,* they who said.

ಹೇಳದ *héḷada,* who or which did not say, ಹೇಳದವನು *héḷadavanu,* he who did not say, &c. &c.

For the union of ಅದು *adu,* with the past and negative participles, See 23, 24.

For the union of ರೆ *re,* ರೂ *rú,* and ಆಗ್ಯೂ *ágyú,* with the past participle, and ಹಾಗೆ *háge,* with the present participle, See the subjunctive mood.

INFINITIVE MOOD.

239. The infinitive mood is governed by the verb which follows it; as,

ನಿಲ್ಲ ಮಾಡಿದನು *nilla mádidanu*, He made to stop.

ನನ್ನನ್ನು ಹೋಗ ಹೇಳಿದನು *nannannu hóga hélidanu*, He told me to go.

240. Occasionally when the infinitive is followed by the present or future tense of ಹೋಗು *hógu*, go, futurity is denoted; as,

ಸೇತುವೆ ಕಟ್ಟ ಹೋಗುತ್ತಾರೆ *sétuve katta hóguttáre*, They are going to build a bridge.

241. When the infinitive is followed by the words ಕೊಡು *kodu*, give, ಕೊಡಿಸು *kodisu*, and ಈಸು *ísu*, to cause to give, permission is denoted; as,

ಮಾಡ ಕೊಡು *máda kodu*, Permit to do.

ಅವರು ಅವನನ್ನು ಹೋಗ ಗೊಡಿಸಲಿಲ್ಲ *avaru avanannu hóga godisalilla*, They did not allow him to go.

ಅವನು ನನ್ನನ್ನು ತನ್ನ ಮನೆಗೆ ಬರಲೀಸನು *avanu nannannu tanna manege baralísanu*, He will not permit me to come to his house.

242. The infinitive in ಲು *lu*, followed by ಒಲ್ಲು *wollu*, is used to denote unwillingness; as,

ನಾನು ಮಾಡಲೊಲ್ಲೆನು *nánu mádalollenu*, I will not (am not willing to) do.

ಹಾಡಲೊಲ್ಲಳು *hádalollalu*, She will not sing.

243. The infinitive in ಲು *lu*, followed by ಇಲ್ಲ *illa*, there is not, denotes negation of a past action; as,

ನಾನು ಕೇಳಲಿಲ್ಲ *nánu kélalilla*, I did not hear; or, I have not heard.

244. When the infinitive is followed by a noun composed of ಉಳ್ಳ *ulla*, and a personal pronoun, obligation or responsibility is denoted; as,

ನಾನು ಕೊಡಲುಳ್ಳವನು *nánu kodalullavanu*, I must (am obliged to) give.

ಅವರು ಹೋಗಲುಳ್ಳವರು *avaru hógalullavaru*, They are the persons who must go.

245. In relating contemporaneous or closely successive actions of the same or different agents, any number of infinitives in ಲು *lu*, may be used in succession, followed by the finite verb expressing the principal or concluding action. The infinitives would be rendered into English by *as, since, whilst, when*, &c. as,

ಲಂಕಾ ಪಟ್ಟಣದಲ್ಲಿ ರಾಕ್ಷಸ ಸೇನೆಗಳು ದುಖ್ಖಿಸಲು, ವಾನರ ಸೇನೆಗಳು ಸಂತೋಷಿಸಲು, ದೇವತೆಗಳು ರಾಮಜಯವನ್ನು ಪ್ರಾರ್ಥಿಸಲು, ಶ್ರೀರಾಮನು ದುರ್ಜನನಾದ ರಾವಣನನ್ನು ಸಂಹರಿಸಿದನು *lanká pattanadalli rákshasa sénegalu dukkhisalu, wánara sénegalu santóṣhisalu, dévategaḷu ráma jayavannu prárthisalu, shrí rámanu durjanaṇáda rávaṇanannu samharisidanu,* Whilst the forces of the giants were grieving in the city of Lanka, the monkey army rejoicing, and the demi-gods praying for the victory of Ràma, the excellent Ràma slew the wicked Ràvana.

246. The past gerund ಆಗಿ *ági,* may be added to these infinitives without affecting the sense; as, ದುಃಖಿಸಲಾಗಿ *dukkhisalági,* ಸಂತೋಷಿಸಲಾಗಿ *santóṣhisalági,* ಪ್ರಾರ್ಥಿಸಲಾಗಿ *prárthisalági.*

IMPERATIVE MOOD.

247. Let, allow, permit, &c. are sometimes expressed by adding ಕೊಡಿಸು *koḍisu,* or ಈಸು *ísu,* cause to give, &c., to the infinitive; as, ಮಾಡ ಗೊಡಿಸು *máḍa-goḍisu,* (or ಮಾಡಲೀಸು *máḍalísu,*) Permit me to do.

248. Verbal nouns in ಉವದು *uvadu,* or ಓಣ *óṇa,* are often used imperatively; as,

ಈ ಕೆಲಸಾ ಮಾಡುವದು *í kelasá máḍuvadu,* Do this work.

ನಾವು ಹೋಗೋಣ *návu hógóṇa* Let us go.

249. Occasionally the future tense of the Affirmative mood is used for the imperative; as,

ನಾನು ಮಾಡುವೆ *nánu máḍuve,* Let me do.

250. The negative imperative is formed by adding ಬೇಡ *béḍa,* to the infinitive; as,

ಮಾಡ ಬೇಡ *máḍa béḍa,* Do not, or, must not do.

ಬರ ಬೇಡ *bara béḍa,* Come not, or, must not come.

251. In commanding inferiors, the particles ಓ *ó,* (mas.) and ಏ *é,* (fem.) are sometimes added to the 2nd per. sing. imperative; as,

ಈ ಕೆಲಸಾ ಮಾಡೋ *í kelasá máḍó,* Do this work.

ಹೋಗೋ *hógó,* Be gone. ಹೇಳೋ *héḷó,* Tell.

ಎಲೇ ಹೆಂಗಸೇ ಇಲ್ಲಿಗೆ ಬಾಯೇ *yelé hengasé illige báyé,* O woman, come here.

252. Except in the 2nd person singular and plural, the form of the imperative is the same.

NEGATIVE MOOD.

253. The Negative mood has only one simple tense, which is either past present or future, according to the context; as,

ಈಗ ಕೊಡರು *íga koḍaru,* They do not (or will not,) now give.

ನಿನ್ನೆ ಹೇಳ್ಳನು *ninne hélanu,* He did not say yesterday.

ನಾಳೆ ಶಿಕ್ಕದು *nále shikkadu,* It will not be to be had to-morrow.

254. Negation is generally expressed by ಇಲ್ಲ *illa,* or ಅಲ್ಲ *alla.*

255. ಇಲ್ಲ *illa,* denies *existence,* and is used with any time, gender, number or person. It may be added to a noun, verbal noun, or infinitive of a verb, and is the negative answer to a question of existence.

256. Added to nouns, ಇಲ್ಲ *illa,* denotes the non-existence of a thing or person, or non-existence in a particular place; as,

ಒಂದೂ ಇಲ್ಲ *wondú illa,* There is not even one.

ಕುದುರೆಯ ಕೊಂಬು ಇಲ್ಲ *kudureya kombu illa,* There is no such thing as a horse's horn.

ಅವನು ಮನೆಯಲ್ಲಿ ಇಲ್ಲ *avanu maneyalli illa,* He is not at home.

ಆ ತೋಟದಲ್ಲಿ ಬಾಳೇ ಮರಗಳು ಇಲ್ಲ *á tótadalli bálé maragalu illa,* There are no plantain trees in that garden.

257. ಇಲ್ಲ *illa,* with a dative or locative case denies possession; as,

ಅವನಿಗೆ ಹಣವಿಲ್ಲ *avanige hanavilla,* He has no money.

ನಿಮ್ಮಲ್ಲಿ ಜ್ಞಾನ ಇಲ್ಲವೋ *nimmalli gnyána illavó,* Have you no wisdom?

ಅವರಿಗೆ ಬುದ್ಧಿ ಇಲ್ಲ ವಿವೇಕವೂ ಇಲ್ಲ *avarige buddhi illa vivékavú illa,* They have neither sense nor discrimination.

258. ಇಲ್ಲ *illa,* is added to verbal nouns; as,

ಇಂಥಾ ಕೆಲಸ ಕಂಡದ್ದೂ ಇಲ್ಲ ಕೇಳಿದ್ದೂ ಇಲ್ಲ *inthá kelasa kandaddú illa, kéliddú illa,* Such a thing as this was never seen or heard of.

ನಾನು ಹೋಗುವದಿಲ್ಲ *nánu hóguvadilla,* I will not go.

ನೀನು ಬರುವದಿಲ್ಲ *nínu baruvadilla,* Thou wilt not come.

ಅವನು (ಅವಳು, ಅದು, ನಾವು, ನೀವು, ಅವರು, ಅವು,) *avanu, (avalu, adu, návu, níru, avaru, avu,)* ಕೊಡುವದಿಲ್ಲ *koduvadilla,* He (she, it, we, ye, they, they neut.) will not give.

259. Examples of ಇಲ್ಲ *illa,* as the negative answer to a question.

ನೀನು ಹಾಗೆ ಹೇಳಿದಿಯೋ *nínu háge hélidiyó,* Did you say so? ಇಲ್ಲ *illa,* No.

ಕೆರೆಯಲ್ಲಿ ನೀರು ಉಂಟೋ *kereyalli níru untó,* Is there any water in the tank? ಇಲ್ಲ *illa,* No.

ಹುಡುಗರು ಮಠಕ್ಕೆ ಹೋಗಿದ್ದಾರೋ *hudugaru mathakke hógiddhdró,* Have the boys gone to school? ಇಲ್ಲ *illa,* No.

260. Negation of quality or nature is expressed by ಅಲ್ಲ *alla,* no; as,

ಇದು ಕಾಗದವೋ *idu kágadavó,* Is this paper? ಅಲ್ಲ *alla,* No (it is something else.)

ಇವನು ನಿನ್ನ ಮಗನೋ *ivanu ninna maganó,* Is this your son? ಅಲ್ಲ *alla,* No, (he is not.)

ಅದು ಪಟ್ಟಣವಲ್ಲ ಚಿಕ್ಕ ಊರು *adu paṭṇavalla chikka úru*, It is not a city, but a small town.

ಇಲ್ಲ *illa*, and ಅಲ್ಲ *alla*, are not interchangeable, and great care must be observed for their correct use.

AFFIRMATIVE MOOD.

261. The Present Tense is commonly used to express future action; as,

ಇಪ್ಪತ್ತು ದಿವಸದಲ್ಲಿ ಬರುತ್ತಾನೆ *ippattu divasadalli baruttáne*, He will come in three weeks.

ತಿಂಗಳಾದ ಮೇಲೆ ಹೋಗುತ್ತೇವೆ *tingaḷáda méle hóguttéve*, We shall go a month hence.

ನಾಳೇ ಕೊಡುತ್ತೀಯೋ *náḷe koḍuttíyó*, Will you give it to-morrow?

These sentences may be rendered, "He is coming," "We are going, &c.

262. The Past Tense is very often used for the future in expressing readiness or immediate action; as,

ಇಲ್ಲಿಗೆ ಬಾ *illige bá*, Come here! ಬಂದೆ *bande*, I shall come, or, I am coming.

ಈ ಕೆಲಸಾ ಮಾಡು *í kelasá máḍu*, Do this work. ಮಾಡಿದೆ *máḍide*, I shall do it (immediately.)

263. The Future Tense is frequently used for the present and past; as,

ಕಾಶಿಯಲ್ಲಿ ಒಬ್ಬ ವಿದ್ವಾಂಸನು ಇರುವನು *káshiyalli wobba vidwámsanu iruvanu*, There lived (or lives) a learned man in Benares.

ಅಂಗ ದೇಶದಲ್ಲಿ ಒಂದು ಪಟ್ಣ ಇರುವದು *anga déshadalli wondu paṭṇa iruvadu*, There was (or is) a city in the Anga country.

ಪೂರ್ವ ಕಾಲದಲ್ಲಿ ಒಬ್ಬ ಅರಸನು ಇರುವನು *púrva kháladalli wobba arasanu iruvanu*, In old time there was a king.

The Future tense is often used to express habitual action; as,

ವರ್ತಕರು ವ್ಯಾಪಾರ ಮಾಡುವರು *wartakaru vyápára máḍuvaru*, Merchants trade.

264. The Contingent Future expresses probability, possibility, and capability; as,

ಮಳೆ ಬಂದೀತು *maḷe bandítu*, It may (is likely to) rain.

ಆದೀತು *ádítu*, Perhaps; it may be so.

ಹೋದಾರು *hódáru*, They will most probably go.

ಹಾಗೆ ಹೇಳ್ಯಾನು *háge héḷyánu*, He will very likely (he may possibly,) say so.

ಆ ಕೆಲಸಾ ಮಾಡೇನು *á kelasá máḍénu*, I can do that work.

POTENTIAL AND SUBJUNCTIVE MOODS.

265. The terms "might," "might have," "would," "would have," &c., and their negatives, are rendered into Canarese by Compound Tenses, and the use of auxiliary verbs; as,

ನೀನು ಆರು ತಿಂಗಳುಗಳ ಕೆಳಗೆ ಕೊಡ ಬೇಕಾಗಿತ್ತು *nínu áru tingaḷugaḷa keḷage koḍa békágittu,* You ought to have given it six months ago.

ಅವರು ಹೋದ ವರುಷದಲ್ಲಿ ಬರ ಬಹುದಾಗಿತ್ತು *avaru hóda varuṣhadalli bara bahudágittu,* They might have come last year.

ನೀನು ಮೊನ್ನೆ ಹೇಳಿದರೆ ನಿನ್ನೆ ಬರುವೆನು *nínu monne héḷidare ninne baruvenu,* If you had told me the day before yesterday, I should have come yesterday.

This sentence may with equal propriety be expressed by,

ನೀನು ಮೊನ್ನೆ ಹೇಳಿದ್ದರೆ ನಿನ್ನೆ ಬಂದಿದ್ದೆನು *nínu monne héḷiddare ninne bandiddenu,* or ಬಂದಿರುವೆನು *bandiruvenu,* or ಬರುತ್ತಿದ್ದೆನು *baruttiddenu,* or ಬರುತ್ತಿರುವೆನು *baruttiruvenu.*

266. The negative is similarly expressed by the use of the negative mood; as,

ನೀನು ಇಲ್ಲಿ ಇದ್ದರೆ ನನ್ನ ಸಹೋದರನು ಸಾಯನು *nínu illi iddare* (or ಇರುತ್ತಿದ್ದರೆ *iruttiddare,*) *nanna sahódaranu sáyanu,* (or ಸಾಯುತ್ತಿದ್ದಿಲ್ಲ *sáyuttiddilla,* or ಸಾಯದೆ ಇರುವನು *sáyade iruvanu,*) If thou hadst been here, my brother would not have died.

CAUSAL VERBS.

267. Causal verbs are necessarily transitive, and govern the accusative case, or the dative of the person and accusative of the thing; as,

ಅವರಿಗೆ ವ್ಯಾಕರಣವನ್ನು ಕಲಿಸಿದನು *avarige vyákaraṇavannu kalisidanu,* He taught them grammar.

ತನ್ನ ಶತ್ರುಗಳನ್ನು ಓಡಿಸಿ ಬಿಟ್ಟನು *tanna shatrigaḷannu wóḍisi biṭṭanu,* He made his enemies to flee.

ಮನೆಯನ್ನು ಕಟ್ಟಿಸಿದನು *maneyannu kaṭṭisidanu,* He had a house built.

Causal verbs take the passive form, and may be treated in every way as regular verbs; as,

ಅವನಿಂದ ವಂಚಿಸಲ್ಪಟ್ಟೆನು *avaninda wanchisalpaṭṭenu,* I was deceived by him.

ಧೊರೆಯ ಅಪ್ಪಣೆಯಿಂದ ಶೂಲಕ್ಕೆ ಹಾಕಿಸಲ್ಪಟ್ಟರು *dhoreya appaṇeyinda shúlakke hákisalpaṭṭaru,* They were impaled by the king's order.

PASSIVE VERBS.

268. Passive verbs are rarely used in Canarese. They are not formed as in English by the addition of the auxiliary verb ಇರು *iru*, Be, to the principal verb, but by adding the word ಪಡು *paḍu*, To experience, to the infinitive ; as,

ದೇವರಿಂದ ಸಕಲವು ಸೃಷ್ಟಿಸಲ್ಪಟ್ಟಿತು *dévarinda sakalavu srishṭisalpaṭṭitu*, Every thing was created by God.

ನಿನ್ನೆ ಹಿಡಿಯಲ್ಪಟ್ಟರು *ninne hiḍiyalpaṭṭaru*, They were seized yesterday.

AUXILIARY AND IRREGULAR VERBS. (115—129.)

ಆಗು *águ*, Become, be.

269. ಆಗಲಿ *ágali*, the 3rd person singular imperative, is used to express assent ; as,

ಹಾಗೆ ಆಗಲಿ *háge ágali*, So be it.

Also for such phrases as, "very well," "be it so," &c.

In certain connections it is equivalent to *either, or* ; as,

ಇದಾಗಲಿ ಅದಾಗಲಿ *idágali, adágali*, Either this or that.

270. Preceded by the dative case, ಆಗು *águ*, expresses suitability, adaptation, &c. ; as,

ನನಗೆ ಆಗುವದಿಲ್ಲ *nanage águvadilla*, It does not suit me.

ಇದು ಕೆಲಸಕ್ಕೆ ಆಗುವದು *idu kelasakke águvadu*, This will be useful ; or, it will do for something.

ಆ ಔಷಧ ಅವನಿಗೆ ಆಗಲಿಲ್ಲ *á oushadha avanige ágalilla*, That medicine did not suit him.

271. Preceded by the instrumental or locative case, it signifies *power, capability*, &c; as,

ನಿನ್ನಿಂದ ಆಗುತ್ತದೋ *ninninda águttadó*, Can you do it?

ನನ್ನಿಂದಲಾಗದು *nannindalágadu*, I cannot.

ಅವನ ಕೈಯಲ್ಲಿ ಈ ಕೆಲಸ ಆಗುವದಿಲ್ಲ *avana keiyalli í kelasa águvadilla*, He is not able to perform this work.

272. The Past Gerund ಆಗಿ *ági*, is a very common affix, and has various significations. The following are some of its uses :—

273. It converts nouns and adjectives into adverbs ; as,

ಬುದ್ಧಿ *buddhi*, sense, ಬುದ್ಧಿಯಾಗಿ *buddhiyági*, sensibly.

ಸುಲಭ *sulabha*, ease, ಸುಲಭವಾಗಿ *sulabhavági*, easily.

ಮಬ್ಬು *mabbu*, dim, dimness, ಮಬ್ಬಾಗಿ *mabbági*, dimly.

274. Words which thus receive an adverbial signification, cannot always be rendered in English by a word ending in *ly*. The sense will be expressed by *for*, *by*, *in*, *like*, *as*, &c.; as,

ಸಾಕ್ಷಿಯಾಗಿ *sákṣhiyági*, as, or for, a witness.

ಮಿತವಾಗಿ *mitavági*, in moderation.

ನಾವು ಈ ಮಾರ್ಗವಾಗಿ ಹೋಗ ಬೇಕು *návu í márgavági hóga béku*, We must go by this road.

ಹುಚ್ಚನಾಗಿ ಮಾತಾಡುತ್ತಾನೆ *huchchanági mátáḍuttáne*, He talks like a fool.

ಅರಸಾಗಿ ರಾಜ್ಯವನ್ನು ಆಳುತ್ತಾನೆ *arasági rájyavannu áḷuttáne*, He rules the country as its king.

275. When added to pronouns, it expresses freeness, spontaneousness, &c.; as,

ನಾನಾಗಿ ಮಾಡಿದೆನು *nánági máḍidenu*, I did of my own accord.

ನೀನಾಗಿ ಹೇಳಿದಿಯೋ *nínági héḷidiyó*, Did you say (it) of your own free will?

ಅವಳಾಗಿ ಓಡಿ ಹೋದಳು *avaḷági wóḍi hódaḷu*, She ran away of her own accord.

ಮನೆ ತಾನಾಗಿ ಬಿತ್ತು *mane tánági bittu*, The house fell of itself.

276. Affixed to the dative case, ಆಗಿ *ági*, signifies, *for*, *in order to*, *on account of*, *in behalf of*, &c.; as,

ವ್ಯಾಪಾರಕ್ಕಾಗಿ ದೇಶಾಂತರಕ್ಕೆ ಹೋದನು *vyápárakkági déshántarakke hódanu*, He went abroad to trade.

ನೋಡುವದಕ್ಕಾಗಿ ಕೂಡಿ ಬಂದರು *nóḍuvadakkági kúḍi bandaru*, They came together to see.

ಆ ಭಯಕ್ಕಾಗಿ ತತ್ತರಿಸಿದರು *á bhayakkági tattarisidaru*, Through fear of that they trembled.

277. Added to an infinitive, ಆಗಿ *ági*, signifies *after*, *when*, *while*, *as*, *in consequence of*, &c.; as,

ಇನ್ನು ಕೆಲ ದಿವಸ ನೋಡಲಾಗಿ ಅವನ ಗುಣ ತಿಳಿಯುತ್ತದೆ *innu kela divasa nóḍalági avana guṇa tiḷiyuttade*, When we have observed him a few days longer, we shall know his disposition. (246.)

278. ಆಗಿ *ági* added to its own infinitive may be rendered "as soon as," "when it took place," &c. as,

ಮಳೆ ಆಗಲಾಗಿ *maḷe ágalági*, As soon as (or when) it rained.

279. ಆಗಿ *ági,* is added to the verbal noun ಎಂಬುವದು *yembuvadu,* or ಎಂಬದು *yembadu,* in marking a quotation; as,

ನನ್ನ ಯಜಮಾನನು ಈ ಕಾಗದ ನಿಮಗೆ ಕೊಡ ಬೇಕು ಎಂಬದಾಗಿ ನನ್ನನ್ನು ಕಳುಹಿಸಿದನು *nanna yajamánanu í kágada nimage koḍa béku yembadágí nannannu kaḷuhisidanu,* My master sent me *saying* that I was to give this letter to you.

280. It is used in forming compound verbs; as,

ಕೆಲಸ ಆಗಿ ಬಂತು *kelasa ágí bantu,* The work is nearly done.

281. In composition with ಇರು *iru,* it expresses nature or quality; as,

ಇದು ಒಳ್ಳೆ ಗ್ರಂಥವಾಗಿದೆಯೋ *idu woḷḷe granthawágideyó,* Is this a good book?

ಸುಮಾರಾಗಿದೆ *sumárágide,* It is middling.

The difference between ಇರು *iru,* and ಆಗಿರು *ágiru,* must be carefully observed.

ಒಳ್ಳೆ ಮನುಷ್ಯನು ಇದ್ದಾನೋ *woḷḷe manuṣhyanu iddhánó,* signifies, Is there such a thing as a good man? or, Does a good man exist? ಒಳ್ಳೆ ಮನುಷ್ಯನಾಗಿದ್ದಾನೋ *woḷḷe manuṣhyanágiddhánó,* means, Is he a good man?

ಬೆಳಕು ಇದೆ *beḷaku ide,* There is light.

ಬೆಳಕಾಗಿದೆ *beḷakágide,* It is light.

ಇರು *iru,* Be.

282. ಇರು *iru,* with a dative case, denotes possession; as,

ಪೂರ್ವದಲ್ಲಿ ನನಗೆ ಆಸ್ತಿ ಇತ್ತು *púrvadalli nanage ásti ittu,* Formerly I had property.

ಈಗ ಕೊಂಚ ಹಣ ಇದೆ *íga koncha haṇa ide,* Now I have a little money.

ಆದರೆ ನನಗೆ ಎಂದೂ ಮಕ್ಕಳು ಇರಲಿಲ್ಲ *ádare nanage yendú makkaḷu iralilla,* But I never had any children.

283. Added to a gerund, it sometimes expresses the habit or continuance of the action; as,

ಓದುತ್ತಾ ಇದ್ದೆನು *wóduttá iddenu,* I was reading, or, in the habit of reading.

ಅನ್ನು *annu,* or ಎನ್ನು *yennu,* Say.

284. The past gerund ಎಂದು *yendu,* is used to mark a quotation of what another has written or said, or the words of a command or message; and answers to the ὅτι in Greek, and inverted commas in English; as,

ಶಾಸ್ತ್ರದಲ್ಲಿ ದೇವರು ಒಬ್ಬನೇ ಎಂದು ಬರೆದದೆ *shástradalli dévaru wobbané yendu baredade,* In the shastra it is written, "God is one."

ಆದರೆ ನೀವು ಹಾಗಲ್ಲ ಎಂದು ಹೇಳುತ್ತೀರಿ *ádare níru hágalla yendu héḷuttíri,* But you say, "Not so."

ಕಳ್ಳತನ ಮಾಡ ಕೂಡದು ಎಂದು ಕಟ್ಟಳೆ ಉಂಟು *kaḷḷatana máḍa kúḍadu yendu kaṭṭaḷe uṇṭu,* There is a command that one must not steal.

ಇಲ್ಲಿಗೆ ಬಾ ಎಂದು ಹೇಳಿದೆನು *illige bá yendu héḷidenu,* I said "Come hither."

ಒಬ್ಬರೂ ಮಾತಾಡ ಬಾರದು ಎಂದು ಅಪ್ಪಣೆ ಮಾಡಿದೆನು *wobbarú mátáḍa bárادu yendu appaṇe máḍidenu,* I commanded that no one should speak.

ಅವನ ಬಳಿಗೆ ಹೋಗಿ ನಾನು ಬರುವದಿಲ್ಲ ಎಂದು ಹೇಳು *avana baḷige hógi nánu baruvadilla yendu héḷu,* Go to him and say that I shall not come.

285. ಎಂದು *yendu,* may be often repeated to mark separate sentences depending on the final verb; as,

ನೀವು ಕೆಲಸವಾಯಿತು ಎಂದೂ ಇವರು ಅದು ನಡೆಯುತ್ತದೆ ಎಂದೂ ಅವರು ಇನ್ನು ಪ್ರಾರಂಭಿಸಲಿಲ್ಲವೆಂದೂ, ಹೇಳಿದ್ದರಿಂದ ನಾನು ಒಬ್ಬರನ್ನೂ ನಂಬಲಾರೆನು, *níru kelasawáyitu yendú, ivaru adu naḍeyuttade yendú, avaru innu prárambhisalillavendú héḷiddarinda nánu wobbarannú nambalárenu,* You say that the work is finished, this man that it is in hand, and that man that it has never been begun, and so I cannot believe one of you. Or, you say, "The work is done;" this man, "It is going on;" and that man, "It is not yet begun;" and therefore I cannot believe any one.

286. ಎಂತ *yenta,* ಎಂತಲು *yentalu,* ಅಂತ *anta,* ಅಂತಲು *antalu,* are frequently used for ಎಂದು *yendu*; as,

ಕುದುರೆಗೆ ತೋಬರೆ ಕಟ್ಟಂತ ಹೇಳು *kuduregé tóbare kaṭṭontu héḷu,* Tell (the horsekeeper) to give the horse his gram.

ಹೋಗಂತ ಅಪ್ಪಣೆ ಕೊಟ್ಟನು *hóganta appaṇe koṭṭanu,* He ordered to go.

287. ಎಂದು *yendu,* is not required when the final verb is ಅನ್ನು *annu,* or ಎನ್ನು *yennu*; as,

ಹೋಯಿತೆಂದನು *hóyitandanu,* "It is gone," he said.

ನೋಡೆಂದನು *nóḍandanu,* "See," said he.

ನನಗೆ ತಿಳಿಯಲಿಲ್ಲ ಅಂದನು *nanage tiḷiyalilla andanu,* He said, "I was not aware." Or, He said that he was not aware.

288. ಅಂತೆ *ante,* is used impersonally for "It is said," "they say;" as,

ಲಿಂಗ ಶೆಟ್ಟಿಯ ಮನೆಯಲ್ಲಿ ಕಳ್ಳತನವಾಯಿತಂತೆ *linga sheṭṭiya maneyalli kaḷḷatanaráyitante,* They say that Linga Shetti's house has been robbed.

ಹತ್ತು ಸಾವಿರ ವರಹಾ ಹೋಯಿತಂತೆ *hattu sávira varahá hóyitante,* It is reported that ten thousand pagodas are gone.

ಕಳ್ಳರು ಶಿಕ್ಕಿದರಂತೆ *kaḷḷaru shikkidarante,* It is said that the thieves have been caught.

ಕೊಳ್ಳು *koḷḷu,* Buy, take.

291. ಕೊಳ್ಳು *koḷḷu,* in all its moods, tenses and persons is added to the Past gerund of other verbs to give them a reflexive signification, similar to the Middle voice in Greek. It denotes that the action is done for the benefit, or on account of, the agent; as,

ಹೊಡೆದನು *hoḍedanu,* He beat (another.) ಹೊಡೆದು ಕೊಂಡನು *hoḍedu-koṇḍanu,* He beat himself, or some other person or thing on his own account.

ಹಣ್ಣು ಹಂಚಿದರು *haṇṇu hanchidaru,* They divided the fruit. ಹಂಚಿ ಕೊಂಡರು *hanchi koṇḍaru,* They divided it among themselves.

ಕಳುಹಿಸಿದರು *kaḷuhisidaru,* They sent (another.) ಕಳುಹಿಸಿ ಕೊಂಡರು *kaḷuhisi koṇḍaru,* They caused themselves to be dismissed.

ಪುಸ್ತಕ ಬರೆದೆನು *pustaka baredenu,* I wrote a book. ಪುಸ್ತಕ ಬರೆದು ಕೊಂಡೆನು *pustaka baredu koṇḍenu,* I wrote a book for myself.

It is very commonly used with causal verbs; as,

ಪುಸ್ತಕ ಬರಿಸಿ ಕೊಂಡೆನು *pustaka barisi koṇḍanu,* I had a book written for myself.

ಸಾಕ್ಷಿ ಹೇಳಿಸಿಕೊಂಡನು *sákshi héḷisi kondanu,* He got evidence given (in his own interest.)

ತನ್ನನ್ನು ತಾನೇ ಕೆಡಿಸಿ ಕೊಂಡನು *tannannu táné keḍisi koṇḍanu,* He ruined himself.

It is occasionally added to ಪಡು *paḍu,* without, however, varying the sense; as, ಸಂತೋಷ ಪಟ್ಟು ಕೊಂಡಳು *santóṣha paṭṭu koṇḍaḷu,* or ಸಂತೋಷ ಪಟ್ಟಳು *santóṣha paṭṭaḷu,* She was glad.

292. The addition of ಕೊಳ್ಳು *koḷḷu,* gives a different signification to some verbs; as,

ನಡೆ *naḍe,* Walk; ನಡೆದು ಕೊಳ್ಳು *naḍedu koḷḷu,* Behave.

Other words are not altered in any way by it; as,

ತಿಳಿದರು *tiḷidaru,* or ತಿಳಿದು ಕೊಂಡರು *tiḷidu koṇḍaru,* They understood.

293. ಕೋ *kó,* is generally used as the second person singular imperative of ಕೊಳ್ಳು *koḷḷu*; as,

ಹಿಡಿದು ಕೋ *hiḍidu kó*, or ಹಿಡುಕೋ *hiḍu kó*, Take hold.

ಪುಸ್ತಕ ಓದಿಕೋ *pustaka wódi kó*, Read the book (for yourself.)

ಬಿಡು *biḍu*, Put forth, &c.

294. ಬಿಡು *biḍu*, added to a gerund, denotes the completeness of the action, and may generally be rendered by *away, off, down, up, out*, &c.; as,

ಹೋಗಿ ಬಿಟ್ಟರು *hógi biṭṭaru*, They went away.

ಅವಳನ್ನು ತಳ್ಳಿ ಬಿಟ್ಟನು *avaḷannu taḷḷi biṭṭanu*, He pushed her away.

ಹೆಂಡತಿಯ ಮೂಗನ್ನು ಕೊಯಿದು ಬಿಟ್ಟನು *heṇḍatiya múgannu koidu biṭṭanu*, He cut off his wife's nose.

ಗುಳಿಗೆ ನುಂಗಿ ಬಿಡ ಬೇಕೇ *guḷige nungi biḍa béké*, Must I swallow down the pill?

ಹುಲ್ಲೆಲ್ಲಾ ತಿಂದು ಬಿಟ್ಟಿತು *hullellá tindu biṭṭitu*, It eat up all the grass.

ಆ ಮಾತು ಬಿಟ್ಟು ಬಿಡು *á mátu biṭṭu biḍu*, Leave out that word.

295. The regular verb ಹಾಕು *háku*, throw, is used in the same sense; as,

ಮಣ್ಣೆಲ್ಲಾ ತೆಗೆದು ಹಾಕಿದ್ಧಾರೆ *maṇṇellá tegedu hákiddhdre*, They have taken out all the earth, &c. &c.

These two verbs are very frequently combined, and have the same signification and use; as,

ಮಣ್ಣೆಲ್ಲಾ ತೆಗೆದು ಹಾಕಿ ಬಿಟ್ಟಿದ್ಧಾರೆ *maṇṇellá tegedu háki biṭṭiddháre*, They have taken out all the earth, &c. &c.

296. Sometimes both ಬಿಡು *biḍu*, and ಹಾಕು *háku*, imply that the agent has no interest in the action; as,

ಅಡಿಗೆ ಮಾಡಿ ಬಿಟ್ಟನು *aḍige mádi biṭṭanu*, He cooked (for another.)

ಬರೆದು ಹಾಕಿದೆನು *baredu hákidenu*, I wrote (it for another.)

ಬರು *baru*, Come.

297. ಬರು *baru*, is of very frequent occurrence, and has a variety of significations; as,

ನಿನಗೆ ವ್ಯಾಕರಣ ಬರುತ್ತದೋ *ninage vyákaraṇa baruttadó*, Do you understand grammar?

ಅವರಿಗೆ ಇನ್ನು ವಿದ್ಯೆ ಬರಲಿಲ್ಲ *avarige innu vidye baralilla*, They are not yet learned.

ನನಗೆ ಬರಹ ಬಾರದು *nanage baraha báradu*, I cannot (do not know to) write.

298. In like manner, it is used with the infinitive (regarded as a verbal noun) of other verbs; as,

ನನಗೆ ಓದ ಬರುವದು *nanage wóda baruvadu,* I can read.

ಅವನಿಗೆ ಬರೆಯ ಬರುವದು *avanige bareya baruvadu,* He can write.

299. ಬರು *baru,* is affixed to gerunds to express *habit, continuance,* or *frequency* of the action; as,

ದೇವರು ಎಲ್ಲರನ್ನು ಕಾಪಾಡುತ್ತಾ ಬರುತ್ತಾನೆ *dévaru yellarannu kápáḍuttá baruttáne,* God continually preserves all.

ಕೊಡುತ್ತಾ ಬಾ *koḍuttá bá,* Continue to give.

ನಾಲ್ಕು ತಿಂಗಳು ಅವನು ನಿತ್ಯವು ಹಾಗೆ ಮಾಡುತ್ತಾ ಬಂದನು *nálku tingaḷu avanu nityavu háge máḍuttá bandanu,* For four months he continued daily to do so.

The meaning is expressed in English by the phrases, "kept on," "keeps on," "goes on," "went on," doing, &c.

In ಹೋಗಿ ಬರುತ್ತೇನೆ *hógi barutténe,* the polite equivalent for, "I am going," on taking leave, the original meaning is dropped; as,

ನಾನು ಹೋಗಿ ಬರಲೋ *nánu hógi baraló,* May I go?

ಹೋಗಿ ಬಾ *hógi bá,* Go.

ಪಡು *paḍu,* Experience.

300. ಪಡು *paḍu,* added to the infinitive of another verb, gives it a passive signification; as,

ಮಾಡು *máḍu,* Do, ಮಾಡಪಡು *máḍa-paḍu,* or ಮಾಡಲ್ಪಡು *máḍal-paḍu,* Be done.

301. Added to nouns of sensation, it turns them into intransitive verbs;

ದುಃಖ ಪಟ್ಟರು *dukkha paṭṭaru,* They sorrowed, experienced grief.

ಆನಂದ ಪಟ್ಟೆನು *ánanda paṭṭenu,* I was glad.

ನೀನು ಭಯ ಪಡಲಿಲ್ಲವೋ *nínu bhaya paḍalillavó,* Were you not afraid?

ದಾಹ ಪಟ್ಟೆವು *dáha paṭṭevu,* We were thirsty.

ಪಡು *paḍu,* is often used in the causal form; as,

ನನಗೆ ಬಹಳವಾಗಿ ದುಃಖ ಪಡಿಸಿದರು *nanage bahaḷawágí dukkha paḍisidaru,* They made me very sorry.

ಅವರನ್ನು ಬೇಸರ ಪಡಿಸ ಬೇಡ *avarannu bésara paḍisa béḍa,* Do not distress them.

ಹೋಗು *hógu,* Go.

302. ಹೋಗು *hógu,* is added to gerunds to express the completeness of the action; and may be rendered by *away, off,* &c.; as,

ಕಳ್ಳರು ಓಡಿ ಹೋದರು *kallaru wódi hódaru*, The thieves ran away.

ಒಡೆದು ಹೋಗಿತ್ತು *wodedu hógittu*, It was broken to pieces.

ಅಡವಿಯೆಲ್ಲಾ ಬೆಂದು ಹೋಯಿತು *adaviyellá bendu hóyitu*, The whole forest was consumed.

ತ್ಯಾವ ಈಗ ಆರಿ ಹೋಯಿತು *tyáva íga ári hóyitu*, The dampness is now dried up.

ಅವನ ಕೈಲಾಗದೆ ಹೋಯಿತು *avana keilágade hóyitu*, He could not do it at all.

ಶಿಕ್ಕದೆ ಹೋದರು *shikkade hóduru*, They could not be found at all.

ಹಣ ಕೊಟ್ಟು ಹೋಯಿತು *hana kottu hóyitu*, The money is all paid up.

303. ಹೋಗು *hógu*, added to the infinitive, sometimes expresses futurity. See 240.

ADVERBS.

304. Adverbs may be formed to an almost unlimited extent by adding ಆಗಿ *ági*, to nouns and adjectives. (130.)

305. The declinable adverbs (See 131—138,) are in many respects treated like nouns and adjectives; as,

ಮುಂಜಾನೆ ಹೋಯಿತು *munjáne hóyitu*, The first watch is past.

ನಿನ್ನಿನ ಕೆಲಸ *ninnina kelasa*, Yesterday's business.

ಅಲ್ಲಿಯ ಜನರು *alliya janaru*, The people of that place.

ನೀವು ಎಲ್ಲಿಯವರು *nívu yelliyavaru*, Of what place are you?

ಈಗಿನ ಕಾಲ *ígina kála*, The present time.

306. Most adverbs precede the words affected by them; and these words may be nouns, adjectives, verbs, participles, gerunds or other adverbs; as,

ಶಾನೆ ನೀರು *sháne níru*, Much water.

ಬಹು ಚಿಕ್ಕ ಮನೆ *bahu chikka mane*, A very little house.

ಚನ್ನಾಗಿ ಓದುತ್ತಾನೆ *channági wóduttáne*, He reads well.

ಬೇಗ ನಡೆಯುವ ಎತ್ತು *béga nadeyuva yettu*, A fast walking ox.

ಅವನಿಗೆ ಬೆಳಗ್ಗೆ ಹೋಗಿ ತಿಳಿಸು *avanige beligye hógi tilisu*, Go in the morning and inform him.

ಬಹು ಜಾಗ್ರತೆಯಾಗಿ ತಕ್ಕೊಂಡು ಹೋದರು *bahu jágrateyági takkondu hódaru*, They carried it away very carefully.

307. ಆಗ *ága*, and ಈಗ *íga*, regarded as adverbs of time, stand alone at the commencement of a sentence or part of a sentence; as,

ಆಗ ಅವರೆಲ್ಲರು ಅತ್ತರು *ága avarellaru attaru*, Then they all wept.

308. ಆಗ *ága,* is affixed to relative participles ; as,

ನಾವು ಹೋಗುವಾಗ *návu hóguvága,* When we go.

ಅವರು ಒಳಗೆ ಪ್ರವೇಶಿಸಿದಾಗ *avaru woḷage pravéshisidága,* When they entered in.

ಕೆರೆಯಲ್ಲಿ ಈಜುತ್ತಿರುವಾಗ *kereyalli íjuttiruvága,* Whilst swimming in the tank.

ನಾನು ಹೊರಟು ಹೋಗಿದ್ದಾಗ *nánu horaṭu hógiddága,* When I had gone out.

309. ಆಗ *ága,* takes the demonstrative and interrogative particles; as,

ಆವಾಗ *ávága,* Then. ಈವಾಗ *ívága,* Now. ಯಾವಾಗ *yávága,* When? ಯಾವಾಗಲೂ *yávágalú,* Always.

310. ಅಂತೆ *ante,* ಹಾಗೆ *hάge,* ಪ್ರಕಾರ *prakára,* ಅಪ್ಪಂದ *appanda,* ನಿಮಿತ್ತ *nimitta,* &c. &c., when affixed to the genitive case, signify *like, as;* as,

ಅದರಂತೆ ಇದು *adarante idu,* This is like that.

ನಿಮ್ಮ ಹಾಗೆ ನಾವು *nimma hάge návu,* We are like you, &c. &c.

311. The same words affixed to relative participles, signify *so that, in order to,* &c.; as,

ತನ್ನ ಸಾಮರ್ಥ್ಯ ತೋರಿಸುವ ಹಾಗೆ ಆಡಿದನು *tanna sámarthya tórisuva hάge aḍidanu,* He acted to display his ability.

ಬಂದಂತೆ ಹೋಯಿತು *bandante hóyitu,* It went as it came.

ಯಾರಿಗೂ ತಿಳಿಯದ ಹಾಗೆ ಮಾಡಿದನು *yárigú tiḷiyada hάge máḍidanu,* He did it so that no one might know.

312. ಅಲ್ಲದೆ *allade,* besides, except, &c. is used after nouns ; as,

ಅವನು ಹಣಗಾರನಲ್ಲದೆ ಧರ್ಮಿಷ್ಠನಾಗಿದ್ದಾನೆ *avanu haṇagáranallade dharmiṣhṭhanágiddháne,* He is a liberal man as well as being rich.

ಇದು ಗಜವಲ್ಲದೆ ಅಜವೋ *idu gajavallade ajavó,* Is this a goat and not an elephant?

313. It is used with pronouns and verbal nouns; as,

ನೀವಲ್ಲದೆ ಇನ್ಯಾರು ದೊಡ್ಡವರು *nívallade inyáru doḍḍavaru,* Who are great people except yourselves (or, if you are not?)

ತಾನು ಹೋಗುವದಲ್ಲದೆ ಮಗನನ್ನು ಕರ ಕೊಂಡು ಹೋಗುತ್ತಾನೆ *tánu hóguvadallade magananu kara koṇḍu hóguttáne,* He will not only go himself, but take his son with him.

ಅವನು ಹುಶಿ ಆಡಿದ್ದಲ್ಲದೆ ನನ್ನನ್ನು ಬೈದನು *avanu hushi áḍiddallade nannannu beidanu,* He not only told a lie, but abused me.

314. It is used after the different moods, tenses and persons of verbs; as,

ನೀನು ಹೀಗೆ ಹೇಳುತ್ತೀ ಅಲ್ಲದೆ ನನಗೆ ಸಹಾಯ ಮಾಡುವದಿಲ್ಲ *nínu híge hél̤uttí allade nanage sahâya mâḍuvadilla*, You not only speak thus, but refuse to help me. Or, You only say so, and do not assist me.

ಎಲ್ಲರು ಮಾತು ಕೊಟ್ಟರಲ್ಲದೆ ಒಬ್ಬರೂ ಏನೂ ಮಾಡಲಿಲ್ಲ *yellaru mâtu koṭṭarallade wobbarú yénú mâḍalilla*, Every body promised, but nobody did any thing.

ನಾವು ಹೋಗುವೆವಲ್ಲದೆ ಮಾಡುವದೇನು *nâvu hóguvevallade mâḍuvadénu*, We shall (may) go, but what can we do?

315. ಅಂತ *anta*, and ಇಂತ *inta*, are affixed to nouns and pronouns with which any thing is compared; as,

ಕುದುರೆಗಿಂತ ಕುರಿ ಚಿಕ್ಕದು *kuduregința kuri chikkadu*, A sheep is less than a horse.

316. In comparing time ಮುಂಚೆ *munche*, &c. are added also; as,

ನಾನು ಕೇಳುವದಕ್ಕಿಂತ ಮುಂಚೆ ಕೊಟ್ಟನು *nânu kél̤uvadakkinta munche koṭṭanu*, He gave before I asked.

317. ಬಹಳ *bahal̤a*, much, is used in forming comparisons; as,

ನನಗಿಂತ ಅವನೇ ಬಹಳ ದೊಡ್ಡ ವಿದ್ವಾಂಸನು *nanaginta avané bahal̤a doḍḍa vidwâmsanu*, He is a much more learned man than I.

318. Many pure adverbs admit the affix ಆಗಿ *âgi*; as, ನುಣ್ಣಗೆ *nuṇṇage*, ನುಣ್ಣಗಾಗಿ *nuṇṇagâgi*.

POSTPOSITIONS.

320. The postpositions generally correspond in meaning with English prepositions. Most of them are affixed to the genitive case; some to the dative; and a few may be affixed to nearly all the cases.

321. The following, from the list, (140, 144) may be added to relative participles, as well as to nouns and pronouns; viz. ಕೂಡ *kúḍa*, ತರುವಾಯ *taruvâya*, ಬಳಿಕ *bal̤ika*, after; ತನಕ *tanaka*, ಪರ್ಯಂತರ *paryantara*, ಮಟ್ಟಿಗೆ *maṭṭige*, ವರಿಗೆ *varige*, until; ಬಗ್ಯೆ *bagye*, ನಿಮಿತ್ತ *nimitta*, for, on account of; ಮೇಲೆ *méle*, upon; ಮುಂಚೆ *munche*, previous to; and ಹೊರ್ತು *hortu*, except; as,

ಅವರು ಬಂದ ಕೂಡಲೇ *avaru banda kúḍalé*, Immediately on their arrival.

ನಾನು ಅಂಗಡಿ ಇಟ್ಟ ತರುವಾಯ *nânu angaḍi iṭṭa taruvâya*, After I had opened shop, &c. &c.

CONJUNCTIONS.

322. ಆದರೆ *ádare,* (subjunctive of ಆಗು *águ,*) *if, but,* &c. is used either alone or subjoined to other words, and has a variety of significations; as,

ಮಲಗಿ ಕೊಂಡೆನು ಆದರೆ ನಿದ್ರೆ ಬರಲಿಲ್ಲ *malagi kondenu ádare nidre baralilla,* I laid myself down, but got no sleep.

ನೀನು ತಪ್ಪು ಮಾಡಿದ್ದುಂಟಾದರೆ ಶಿಕ್ಷೆ ತಪ್ಪದು *nínu tappu mádiddun̤tádare shikṣhe tappadu,* If you have committed a fault, you cannot escape punishment.

ನಾನು ಸುಳ್ಳು ಹೇಳಿದೆನಾದರೆ ನನ್ನ ನಾಲಿಗೆ ಕೊಯಿದು ಹಾಕ ಬಹುದು *nánu suḷḷu héḷidenádare nanna nálige koyidu háka bahudu,* If I have told a lie, you may cut my tongue out.

323. It is used to signify *as for, with respect to,* &c.; as,

ಅವರು ಹಾಗೆ ಮಾಡ ಬಹುದು ನಾವಾದರೆ ಮಾಡ ಕೂಡದು *avaru háge máḍa-bahudu, náváddare máḍa kúḍadu,* They may do so; as for us we cannot.

324. ಆದರೂ *ádarú,* (ಆದರೆ *ádare,* with ಊ *ú,*) is used alone for *yet, nevertheless, notwithstanding;* as,

ನೀವು ಚನ್ನಾಗಿ ಮಾತಾಡುತ್ತೀರಿ ಆದರೂ ನೀವು ನಡೆಯುವದಿಲ್ಲ *nívu channági mátáḍuttíri ádarú nívu naḍeyuvadilla,* You talk very well, yet you do not walk (accordingly.)

ನೀವು ಹೇಳಿದ್ದೆಲ್ಲಾ ಸರಿಯೇ ಆದರೂ ಬೇರೆ ಒಂದು ಕೆಲಸ ಅದೆ *nívu héḷiddellá sariyé ádarú bére wondu kelasa ade,* All you say is very well; nevertheless there is another point (to be taken into account.)

325. As a disjunctive, ಆದರೂ *ádarú,* is added to nouns, verbal nouns and pronouns of any case except the genitive and vocative: as,

ನೀನಾದರೂ ಅವನಾದರೂ ಮಾಡಿರ ಬೇಕು *nínádarú avanádarú máḍira béku,* Either you or he must have done it.

ನಾನು ವೇದವನ್ನಾದರೂ ಪುರಾಣವನ್ನಾದರೂ ಓದಲಿಲ್ಲ *nánu védavannádarú, puráṇavanndádarú wódalilla,* I have not read either véda or purána.

ಈ ಸ್ಥಳಕ್ಕಾದರೂ ಆ ಸ್ಥಳಕ್ಕಾದರೂ ಹೋಗ ಬೇಡ *í sthaḷakkádarú á sthaḷakkádarú hóga béḍa,* Do not go to either this place or that.

ಮಾಡುವದಾದರೂ ಸರಿಯೇ ಬಿಡುವದಾದರೂ ಸರಿಯೇ *máḍuvaddádarú sariyé, biḍuvadádarú sariye,* It will be right whether you do it or let it alone.

326. ಆದರೂ *ádarú,* is used to express *even, at any rate, at least;* as,

ನೀವಾದರೂ ಬರ ಬೇಕು *nívádarú bara béku,* You must come at any rate. Or, you at least must come.

ನನಗೆ ಒಂದಾದರೂ ಇಲ್ಲ *nanage wondádarú illa,* I have not even one.

327. ಆದರೂ *ádarú,* added to interrogatives, expresses the sense of *so-ever, some;* as,

ಯಾರು *yáru,* who, ಯಾರಾದರೂ *yárádarú,* Some one, any one whosoever.

ಯಾವ *yáva,* who, which or what, ಯಾವನಾದರೂ *yávanádarú,* Some one, any one, whosoever.

ಯಾವದಾದರೂ *yávadádarú,* Whatsoever.

ಯಾವ ಸ್ಥಳದಲ್ಲಾದರೂ *yáva sthaḷadallyádarú,* In what place soever.

ಯಾವಾಗ *yáváya,* when, ಯಾವಾಗಾದರೂ *yáváyádarú,* or ಯಾವಾಗಲಾದರೂ *yávágalddarú,* Whensoever, at some time, at any time.

328. ಎಲ್ಲಿ *yelli,* where, ಎಲ್ಲಿಯಾದರೂ *yelliyádarú,* Some where, any where.

ಎಲ್ಲಿಗಾದರೂ *yelligádarú,* Some whither, any whither.

ಎಲ್ಲಿಂದಲಾದರೂ *yellindaládarú,* Whencesoever.

329. ಏನು *yénu,* what, ಏನಾದರೂ *yénddarú,* Something, any thing, whatsoever.

330. ಹ್ಯಾಗೆ *hyáge,* how, ಹ್ಯಾಗಾದರೂ *hyágddarú,* By some means, somehow.

331. ಆದಾಗ್ಯೂ *ádágyú,* is the same in all respects as ಆದರೂ *ádarú.*

332. ಆಗಲಿ *ágali,* either, or, &c., is affixed to nouns in nearly all their cases; as,

ದೊಡ್ಡದಾಗಲಿ ಚಿಕ್ಕದಾಗಲಿ *doḍḍadágali chikkadágali,* Either a large or small one.

ಮಣ್ಣಾಗಲಿ ಕಲ್ಲಾಗಲಿ *maṇṇágali kallágali,* Either earth or stone.

ಹೊಲದಲ್ಲ್ಯಾಗಲಿ ತೋಟದಲ್ಲ್ಯಾಗಲಿ *holadallyágali tóṭadallyágali,* Either in field or garden.

333. ಆದದರಿಂದ *ádadarinda,* or ಆದ್ದರಿಂದ *áddarinda,* (ಆದ *áda,* and ಅದರಿಂದ *adarinda,*) therefore, expresses a consequence; as,

ನನ್ನನ್ನು ವಿಚಾರಿಸುವವರು ಯಾರೂ ಇಲ್ಲ ಆದ್ದರಿಂದ ನೀವೇ ಕಾಪಾಡ ಬೇಕು *nannannu, vichárisuvavaru yárú illa; áddarinda nívé kápáḍa béku,* There is no one who will take any interest in me; therefore you must take care of me.

334. ಊ *ú,* is used as a copulative of words and sentences; as,

ನೀವೂ ನಾವೂ *nívú návú,* You and I.

ಬರುವದೂ ಹೋಗುವದೂ *baruvadú hóguvadú,* Coming and going.

ಒಬ್ಬನಿಗೆ ವಸ್ತ್ರವಿಲ್ಲವೆಂದೂ, ಮತ್ತೊಬ್ಬನಿಗೆ ಅನ್ನವಿಲ್ಲವೆಂದೂ, ಹೇಳುತ್ತಾನೆ *wobbanige vastravillavendú, mattobbanige annavillavendú héḷuttáne,* He says, that one has no clothes, and the other no food.

335. ಊ *ú,* followed by ಇಲ್ಲ *illa,* or ಅಲ್ಲ *alla,* signifies *neither, nor;* as,

ಅವನು ಇದನ್ನೂ ಮಾಡುವದಿಲ್ಲ ಅದನ್ನೂ ಮಾಡುವದಿಲ್ಲ *avanu idannú máḍuvadilla adannú máḍuvadilla,* He will do neither this nor that.

ಇದು ಸಮುದ್ರವೂ ಅಲ್ಲ ನದಿಯೂ ಅಲ್ಲ ಕೆರೆಯೇ *idu samudravú alla, nadiyú alla kereyé,* This is neither a sea nor a river, but a lake.

336. ಊ *ú* ಇಲ್ಲ *illa,* or ಅಲ್ಲ *alla,* with an interrogative, gives a universal negation; as,

ಎಲ್ಲಿ *yelli,* where? ಎಲ್ಲಿಯೂ ಇಲ್ಲ *yelliyú illa,* No where.

ಎಂದು *yendu,* when? ಎಂದೂ ಇಲ್ಲ *yendú illa,* Never.

ಯಾರು *yáru,* who? ಯಾರೂ ಇಲ್ಲ *yárú illa,* There is no one. ಯಾರೂ ಅಲ್ಲ *yárú alla,* It is no one.

ಯಾವದು *yávadu,* which? ಯಾವದೂ ಇಲ್ಲ *yávadú illa,* None at all.

ಹ್ಯಾಗೆ *hyáge,* how? ಹ್ಯಾಗೂ ಇಲ್ಲ *hyágú illa,* In no way, by no means whatsoever.

PARTICLES.

337. ಆ *á,* ಏ *é,* ಓ *ó,* are affixed as interrogative particles; as,

ಹಾಗೆ ಹೇಳಿದಿಯಾ *háge héḷidiyá,* Did you say so?

ನಾನು ಹೋಗಲೇ *nánu hógalé,* ಹೋಗಲೋ *hógaló,* Shall I go?

338. ಏ *é,* is emphatic; as,

ಅದೇ ಮಾತು *adé mátu,* That very word.

ನಾವು ಒಳ್ಳೇದನ್ನೇ ಮಾಡ ಬೇಕು *návu woḷḷédanné máḍa béku,* We must do only good.

339. ಓ *ó,* is very commonly used to express doubt; as,

ಅವರು ಬಂದರೋ ಏನೋ *avaru bandaró yénó,* Whether they have come or not (I cannot tell.)

ಎಲ್ಲಿಗೆ ಹೋಗಿದ್ದಾರೆ *yellige hógiddháre,* Whither have they gone? ಎಲ್ಲಿಗೋ *yelligó,* Whither (I know not.)

ಎಲ್ಲಿಗೆ ಹೋಗಿದ್ದಾರೋ *yellige hógiddháró,* Whither they have gone (I cannot tell.)

ಯಾರೋ ಹೇಳಿದರು *yáró héḷidaru,* Some one or another said it.

ಹ್ಯಾಗಾಯಿತು *hyágáyitu,* How did it happen? ಹ್ಯಾಗೋ *hyágó,* How (I know not.)

ಮನುಷ್ಯರೆಲ್ಲರು ಪಾಪಾತ್ಮರು *manuṣhyarellaru pápátmaru,* All men are sinners. ನೀವೋ *nívó,* You? (What are you then?)

ನಾವೋ? ನಾವೇ ಪಾಪಾತ್ಮರು *návó, návé pápátmaru,* We? We also are sinners.

APPENDIX.

340. GRAMMATICAL TERMS.

Letter	ವರ್ಣ *warṇa.*
Vowel	ಸ್ವರ *swara.*
Short	ಹ್ರಸ್ವ *hraswa.*
Long	ದೀರ್ಘ *dírgha.*
Consonant	ವ್ಯಂಜನ *vyanjana.*
Junction of letters	ಸಂಧಿ *sandhi.*
Elision ,,	ಲೋಪ *lópa.*
Insertion ,,	ಆಗಮ *ágama.*
Change ,,	ಆದೇಶ *ádésha.*
Syllable ,,	ಅಕ್ಷರ *akṣhara.*
Word (part of speech)	ಶಬ್ದ *shabda.*
Pure Canarese	ದೇಶ್ಯ *déshya.*
Pure Sanscrit	ತತ್ಸಮ *tatsama.*
Corrupted Sanscrit	ತದ್ಭವ *tadbhava.*
Foreign words	ಅನ್ಯದೇಶ್ಯ *anya-déshya.*
Ungrammatical forms.	ಗ್ರಾಮ್ಯ *grámya.*
Uninflected word (Crude state)	ಪ್ರಕೃತಿ *prakṛiti.*
Inflected word	ಪದ *pada.*
Affix	ಪ್ರತ್ಯಯ *pratyaya.*
Sentence	ವಾಕ್ಯ *vákya.*
Noun	ನಾಮವಾಚಕ *náma-wáchaka.*
Gender	ಲಿಂಗ *linga.*
Masculine	ಪುಲ್ಲಿಂಗ *pullinga.*
Feminine	ಸ್ತ್ರೀಲಿಂಗ *strí-linga.*
Neuter	ನಪುಂಸಕಲಿಂಗ *napumsaka-linga.*
Number	ವಚನ *wachana.*
Singular	ಏಕವಚನ *yéka-wachana.*

Plural	ಬಹುವಚನ *bahu-wachana.*
Case	ವಿಭಕ್ತಿ *vibhakti.*
Nominative (1st.)	ಪ್ರಥಮೆ *prathame.*
Accusative (2nd.)	ದ್ವಿತೀಯೆ *dwitiye.*
Instrumental (3rd.)	ತೃತೀಯೆ *tṛitiye.*
Dative (4th)	ಚತುರ್ಥಿ *chaturthi.*
Ablative (5th)	ಪಂಚಮಿ *panchami.*
Genitive (6th)	ಷಷ್ಠಿ *ṣhaṣhṭi.*
Locative (7th)	ಸಪ್ತಮಿ *saptami.*
Vocative (8th)	ಸಂಬೋಧನೆ *sambódhane.*
Declension	ರೂಪ *rúpa.*
Noun of relationship	ಬಂಧುವಾಚಕ *bandhu-wáchaka.*
Adjective	ಗುಣವಾಚಕ *guṇa-wáchaka.*
Numeral	ಸಂಖ್ಯಾವಾಚಕ *sankhyá-wáchaka.*
Pronoun	ಸರ್ವನಾಮ *sarva-náma.*
Verb	ಕ್ರಿಯಾಪದ *kriyápada.*
Root (verbal)	ಧಾತು *dhátu.*
Agent (nom: to verb)	ಕರ್ತೃ *kartṛi.*
Object (governed by verb)	ಕರ್ಮ *karma.*
Person	ಪುರುಷ *puruṣha.*
1st	ಉತ್ತಮ *uttama.*
2nd	ಮಧ್ಯಮ *madhyama.*
3rd	ಪ್ರಥಮ *prathama.*
Inflected forms of the verb.	ಆಖ್ಯಾತರೂಪಗಳು *ákhyáta-rúpagaḷu.*
Mood	ರೂಪ *rúpa.*
Imperative	ವಿಧಿ *vidhi.*
Negative	ನಿಷೇಧ *niṣhédha.*
Affirmative	ನಿಶ್ಚಯರೂಪ *nishchaya-rúpa.*
Subjunctive	ಸಂಶಯರೂಪ *samshaya-rúpa.*
Tense	ಕಾಲ *kála.*
Present	ವರ್ತಮಾನ *wartamána.*
Past	ಭೂತ *bhúta.*
Future	ಭವಿಷ್ಯತ್ತು *bhaviṣhyattu.*
Uninflected forms of the verb	ಅವ್ಯಯರೂಪಗಳು *avyaya-rúpagaḷu.*

Infinitive Mood	ಭಾವರೂಪ *bháva-rúpa.*
Participle	ಕ್ರಿಯಾನ್ಯೂನ *kriyá-nyúna.*
Gerund	ಶಬ್ದನ್ಯೂನ *shabda-nyúna.*
Compound Gerund	ಸಂಯುಕ್ತಶಬ್ದನ್ಯೂನ *samyukta-shabda-nyúna.*
Active verb.	ಸಕರ್ಮಕ್ರಿಯಾಪದ *sakarma kriyápada.*
Neuter verb.	ಅಕರ್ಮ ಕ್ರಿಯಾಪದ *akarma kriyápada.*
Regular verb.	ಕ್ರಮವಾದ ಕ್ರಿಯಾಪದ *kramawáda kriyápada.*
Irregular.	ವಿಕೃತ ಕ್ರಿಯಾಪದ *vikṛita kriyápada.*
Defective.	ಉಪಪದ ಕ್ರಿಯಾಪದ *upapada kriyápada.*
Reflective.	ಸ್ವಾರ್ಥ ಕ್ರಿಯಾಪದ *swártha kriyápada.*
Passive.	ಕರ್ಮಣಿ ಕ್ರಿಯಾಪದ *karmaṇi kriyápada.*
Causal.	ಪ್ರೇರಣ ಕ್ರಿಯಾಪದ *préraṇa kriyápada.*
Indeclinable words.	ಅವ್ಯಯಗಳು *avyayagaḷu.*
Postposition.	ವಿಭಕ್ತ್ಯಾವ್ಯಯ *vibhaktávyaya.*
Adverb joined to nouns or pronouns.	ಗುಣವಿಶೇಷಣ *guṇa vishéṣhaṇa.*
,, verbs.	ಕ್ರಿಯಾವಿಶೇಷಣ *kriyá vishéṣhaṇa.*
Conjunction.	ಸಂಬಂಧಕಾವ್ಯಯ *sambandhakávyaya.*
Interjection, calling another.	ಸಂಬುದ್ಧ್ಯಾವ್ಯಯ *sambuddhávyaya.*
Exclamation of wonder.	ಅತಿಶಯಾವ್ಯಯ *atishayávyaya.*
Derivative noun.	ತದ್ಧಿತ ಪ್ರತ್ಯಯ *taddhita pratyaya.*
Verbal noun.	ಕ್ರಿಯಾವಾಚಕ or ಕೃತ್ಪ್ರತ್ಯಯ *kriyáwáchaka,* or *kṛitpratyaya.*
Compound noun.	ಸಮಾಸಪದ *samása pada.*
Syntax.	ಪ್ರಯೋಗ *prayóga.*
Parsing.	ಪದವಿಭಾಗ ಮಾಡುವದು *pada vibhága máḍuvadu.*
Prosody.	ಕವಿತ್ವ ಲಕ್ಷಣ *kavitwa lakṣhaṇa.*
Metre.	ಛಂದಸ್ಸು *chhandassu.*
Verse	ಶ್ಲೋಕ *shlóka.*
Line of a verse	ಪಾದ *páda.*
Rhyme	ಪ್ರಾಸ *prása.*

341. CARDINAL NUMBERS.

ಒಂದು *wondu,*	೧	1
ಎರಡು *yeraḍu,*	೨	2
ಮೂರು *múru,*	೩	3
ನಾಲ್ಕು *nálku,*	೪	4
ಐದು *eidu,*	೫	5
ಆರು *áru,*	೬	6
ಏಳು *yéḷu,*	೭	7
ಎಂಟು *yeṇṭu,*	೮	8
ಒಂಭತ್ತು *wombhattu,*	೯	9
ಹತ್ತು *hattu,*	೧೦	10
ಹನ್ನೊಂದು *hannondu,*	೧೧	11
ಹನ್ನೆರಡು *hanneraḍu,*	೧೨	12
ಹದಿಮೂರು *hadimúru,*	೧೩	13
ಹದಿನಾಲ್ಕು *hadinálku,*	೧೪	14
ಹದಿನೈದು *hadineidu,*	೧೫	15
ಹದಿನಾರು *hadináru,*	೧೬	16
ಹದಿನೇಳು *hudinéḷu,*	೧೭	17
ಹದಿನೆಂಟು *hadineṇṭu,*	೧೮	18
ಹತ್ತೊಂಭತ್ತು *hattombhattu,*	೧೯	19
ಇಪ್ಪತ್ತು *ippattu,*	೨೦	20
ಇಪ್ಪತ್ತೊಂದು *ippattondu,*	೨೧	21
ಇಪ್ಪತ್ತೆರಡು *ippatteraḍu,*	೨೨	22
ಇಪ್ಪತ್ತುಮೂರು *ippattu-múru,*	೨೩	23
ಇಪ್ಪತ್ತುನಾಲ್ಕು *ippattunálku,*	೨೪	24
ಇಪ್ಪತ್ತೈದು *ippatteidu,*	೨೫	25
ಇಪ್ಪತ್ತಾರು *ippattáru,*	೨೬	26
ಇಪ್ಪತ್ತೇಳು *ippattéḷu,*	೨೭	27
ಇಪ್ಪತ್ತೆಂಟು *ippatteṇṭu,*	೨೮	28
ಇಪ್ಪತ್ತೊಂಭತ್ತು *ippattombhattu,*	೨೯	29
ಮೂವತ್ತು *múvattu,*	೩೦	30
ನಾಲ್ವತ್ತು *nálvattu,*	೪೦	40
ಐವತ್ತು *eivattu,*	೫೦	50
ಅರವತ್ತು *aravattu,*	೬೦	60
ಎಪ್ಪತ್ತು *yeppattu,*	೭೦	70

ಎಂಭತ್ತು *yembhattu,*	೮೦	80
ತೊಂಭತ್ತು *tombhattu,*	೯೦	90
ನೂರು *núru,*	೧೦೦	100
ನೂರೊಂದು *núrondu,*	೧೦೧	101
ನೂರಹತ್ತು *núrahattu,*	೧೧೦	110
ಇನ್ನೂರು *innúru,*	೨೦೦	200
ಮುನ್ನೂರು *munnúru,*	೩೦೦	300
ನಾನೂರು *nánúru,*	೪೦೦	400
ಐನೂರು *einúru,*	೫೦೦	500
ಆರುನೂರು *árunúru,*	೬೦೦	600
ಏಳ್ನೂರು *yéḷnúru,*	೭೦೦	700
ಎಂಟುನೂರು *yeṇṭunúru,*	೮೦೦	800
ಒಂಭಯಿನೂರು *wombhainúru,*	೯೦೦	900
ಸಾವಿರ *sávira,*	೧,೦೦೦	1,000
ಸಾವಿರದೊಂದು *sáviradondu,*	೧,೦೦೧	1,001
ಸಾವಿರದಹತ್ತು *sáviradahattu,*	೧,೦೧೦	1,010
ಸಾವಿರದನೂರು *sáviradanúru,*	೧,೧೦೦	1,100
ಹತ್ತುಸಾವಿರ *hattusávira,*	೧೦,೦೦೦	10,000
ಲಕ್ಷ *lakṣha,*	೧,೦೦,೦೦೦	1,00,000
ಕೋಟಿ *kóṭi,*	೧,೦೦,೦೦,೦೦೦	1,00,00,000

342. ORDINAL NUMBERS.

The ordinal numbers are formed by adding the affix ಅನೇ *ané,* to the Cardinal numbers.

ಒಂದನೇ *wondané,*
ಮೊದಲನೇ *modaḷané,* } ೧ನೇ 1st.
ಎರಡನೇ *yeraḍané,* ೨ನೇ 2nd.
ಮೂರನೇ *múrané,* ೩ನೇ 3rd.
ನಾಲ್ಕನೇ *nálkané,* ೪ನೇ 4th.
&c. &c. &c. &c.

343. Multiplicative numbers are formed by adding to the cardinal numbers, ಅಷ್ಟು *ashṭu,* so much, ಮಡಿ *maḍi,* fold, ಪಾಲು *pálu,* part, &c. as,

ಎರಡಷ್ಟು *yeraḍashṭu,* Twice as much.
ಇಮ್ಮಡಿ *im-maḍi,* Two-fold, double.
ಮೂರು ಪಾಲು *múru pálu,* Three parts.
&c. &c.

344. Repetition is expressed by adding ಆವರ್ತಿ *ávarti,* ಬಾರಿ *bári,* ಸಾರಿ *sári,* ಸರ್ತಿ *sarti,* ಸರದಿ *saradi,* ಸಲ *sala,* ವಂತಿಗೆ *vantige,* (dative case of ಒಂತು *wontu,*) all signifiying *time, turn, rotation*; as,

ಮೂರಾವರ್ತಿ *múrávarti,* three times.
ನಾಲ್ಕು ಬಾರಿ *nálku bári,* four times, &c. &c.

345. The principal Fractions, with their signs, are,

—	ವೀಸ *visa,*	1-16
=	ಬೇಳೆ *béḷe,*	1-8
I	ಕಾಲು *kálu,*	$\frac{1}{4}$
II	ಅರೆ *are,*	$\frac{1}{2}$
III	ಮುಕ್ಕಾಲು *mukkálu,*	$\frac{3}{4}$

346. Names of the years in the Hindu cycle.

1	ಪ್ರಭವ *prabhava.*	31	ಹೇವಳಂಬಿ *hevaḷambi.*
2	ವಿಭವ *vibhava.*	32	ವಿಳಂಬಿ *viḷambi.*
3	ಶುಕ್ಲ *shukla.*	33	ವಿಕಾರಿ *vikári.*
4	ಪ್ರಮೋದೂತ *pramódúta.*	34	ಶಾರ್ವರಿ *shárvari.*
5	ಪ್ರಜೋತ್ಪತ್ತಿ *prajótpatti.*	35	ಪ್ಲವ *plava.*
6	ಆಂಗೀರಸ *ángírasa.*	36	ಶುಭಕೃತು *shubhakṛitu.*
7	ಶ್ರೀಮುಖ *shrímukha.*	37	ಶೋಭಕೃತು *shóbhakṛitu.*
8	ಭಾವ *bháva.*	38	ಕ್ರೋಧಿ *kródhi.*
9	ಯುವ *yuva.*	39	ವಿಶ್ವಾವಸು *vishvávasu.*
10	ಧಾತು *dhátu.*	40	ಪರಾಭವ *parábhava.*
11	ಈಶ್ವರ *íshvara.*	41	ಪ್ಲವಂಗ *plavanga.*
12	ಬಹುಧಾನ್ಯ *bahudhánya.*	42	ಕೀಲಕ *kílaka.*
13	ಪ್ರಮಾದಿ *pramádi.*	43	ಸೌಮ್ಯ *soumya.*
14	ವಿಕ್ರಮ *vikrama.*	44	ಸಾಧಾರಣ *sádháraṇa.*
15	ವಿಷು *viṣhu.*	45	ವಿರೋಧಿಕೃತು *viródhikṛitu.*
16	ಚಿತ್ರಭಾನು *chitrabhánu.*	46	ಪರಿಧಾವಿ *paridhávi.*
17	ಸ್ವಭಾನು *swabhánu.*	47	ಪ್ರಮಾದೀಚ *pramádícha.*
18	ತಾರಣ *táraṇa.*	48	ಆನಂದ *ánanda.*
19	ಪಾರ್ಥಿವ *párthiva.*	49	ರಾಕ್ಷಸ *rákṣhasa.*
20	ವ್ಯಯ *vyaya.*	50	ನಳ *naḷa.*
21	ಸರ್ವಜಿತು *sarvajitu.*	51	ಪಿಂಗಳ *pingaḷa.*
22	ಸರ್ವಧಾರಿ *sarvadhári.*	52	ಕಾಳಯುಕ್ತಿ *káḷayukti.*
23	ವಿರೋಧಿ *viródhi.*	53	ಸಿದ್ಧಾರ್ಥಿ *siddhárthi.*
24	ವಿಕೃತಿ *vikṛiti.*	54	ರೌದ್ರಿ *roudri.*
25	ಖರ *khara.*	55	ದುರ್ಮತಿ *durmati.*
26	ನಂದನ *nandana.*	56	ದುಂದುಭಿ *dundubhi.*
27	ವಿಜಯ *vijaya.*	57	ರುಧಿರೋದ್ಗಾರಿ *rudhiródgári.*
28	ಜಯ *jaya.*	58	ರಕ್ತಾಕ್ಷಿ *raktákṣhi.*
29	ಮನ್ಮಥ *manmatha.*	59	ಕ್ರೋಧನ *kródhana.*
30	ದುರ್ಮುಖಿ *durmukhi.*	60	ಕ್ಷಯ *kṣhaya,* or ಅಕ್ಷಯ *akṣhaya.*

347. MONTHS.

ಚೈತ್ರ *cheitra,* March—April.
ವೈಶಾಖ *veishákha,* April—May.
ಜೇಷ್ಠ *jéshṭha,* May—June.
ಆಷಾಢ *áshádha,* June—July.
ಶ್ರಾವಣ *shrávaṇa,* July—August.
ಭಾದ್ರಪದ *bhádrapada,* August—September.
ಆಶ್ವೀಜ *áshwíja,* September—October.
ಕಾರ್ತೀಕ *kártíka,* October—November.
ಮಾರ್ಗಶಿರ *márgashira,* November—December.
ಪುಷ್ಯ *pushya,* December—January.
ಮಾಘ *mágha,* January—February.
ಫಾಲ್ಗುಣ *phálguṇa,* February—March.

348. The year is divided into six Seasons.

ವಸಂತ ಋತು *vasanta ṛitu,* Spring, comprising ಚೈತ್ರ *cheitra,* and ವೈಶಾಖ *veishákha.*

ಗ್ರೀಷ್ಮ ಋತು *gríshma ṛitu,* Hot season, ಜೇಷ್ಠ *jéshṭha,* and ಆಷಾಢ *áshádha.*

ವರ್ಷ ಋತು *varsha ṛitu,* Rainy season, ಶ್ರಾವಣ *shrávaṇa,* and ಭಾದ್ರಪದ *bhádrapada.*

ಶರದೃತು *sharad ṛitu,* Autumn, ಆಶ್ವೀಜ *áshwíja,* and ಕಾರ್ತೀಕ *kártíka.*

ಹಿಮಂತ ಋತು *himanta ṛitu,* Winter, ಮಾರ್ಗಶಿರ *márgashira,* and ಪುಷ್ಯ *pushya.*

ಶಿಶಿರ ಋತು *shishira ṛitu,* Cool season, ಮಾಘ *mágha,* and ಫಾಲ್ಗುಣ *phálguṇa.*

349. The day of 24 English hours is divided into sixty ಘಳಿಗೆ *ghaḷige,* of 24 minutes each.

350. The days of the week are called after the planets.

1.	ಭಾನುವಾರ *bhánuwára,*	Sunday from	ಭಾನು	Sun.
	ರವಿವಾರ *raviwára,*	do. „	ರವಿ	do.
	ಆದಿತ್ಯವಾರ *ádityawára,*	do. „	ಆದಿತ್ಯ	do.
	ಆದಿವಾರ *ádiwára,*	do. „	ಆದಿ	First.
2.	* ಸೋಮವಾರ *sómawára,*	Monday „	ಸೋಮ	Moon.
	ಇಂದುವಾರ *induwára,*	do. „	ಇಂದು	do.
	ಚಂದ್ರವಾರ *chandrawára,*	do. „	ಚಂದ್ರ	do.
3.	* ಮಂಗಳವಾರ *mangaḷawára,*	Tuesday „	ಮಂಗಳ	Mars.
	ಕುಜವಾರ *kujawára,*	do. „	ಕುಜ	do.
	ಅಂಗಾರಕವಾರ *angárakawára,*	do. „	ಅಂಗಾರಕ	do.
	ಭೌಮವಾರ *bhoumawára,*	do. „	ಭೌಮ	do.

* These are generally used.

4.	* ಬುಧವಾರ *budhawára,*	Wednesday		ಬುಧ	Mercury.
	ಸೌಮ್ಯವಾರ *soumyawára,*	do.		ಸೌಮ್ಯ	do.
5.	* ಬೃಹಸ್ಪತಿವಾರ *bṛihaspatiwára,*	Thursday		ಬೃಹಸ್ಪತಿ	Jupiter.
	ಗುರುವಾರ *guruwára,*	do.	,,	ಗುರು	do.
6.	ಶುಕ್ರವಾರ *shukrawára,*	Friday	,,	ಶುಕ್ರ	Venus.
	ಭಾರ್ಗವವಾರ *bhárgavawára,*	do.	,,	ಭಾರ್ಗವ	do.
7.	ಶನಿವಾರ *shaniwára,*	Saturday	,,	ಶನಿ	Saturn.
	ಸ್ಥಿರವಾರ *sthirawára,*	do.	,,	ಸ್ಥಿರ	do.
	ಮಂದವಾರ *mandawára,*	do.		ಮಂದ	do.

* These are generally used.